HOLLYWOOD
behind the LENS

Gloria Swanson, promoting her comeback vehicle "Sunset Boulevard," installs a namesake street sign in Beverly Hills (1950).

HOLLYWOOD
behind the LENS

treasures from the

BISON
ARCHIVES

MARC WANAMAKER
AND STEVEN BINGEN

LYONS
PRESS

Essex, Connecticut

LYONS
PRESS

An imprint of Globe Pequot, the trade division of
The Rowman & Littlefield Publishing Group, Inc.
4501 Forbes Blvd., Ste. 200
Lanham, MD 20706
www.rowman.com

Distributed by NATIONAL BOOK NETWORK

British Library Cataloguing in Publication Information available

Library of Congress Cataloging-in-Publication Data
Names: Wanamaker, Marc, author. | Bingen, Steven, author. | Bison Archives.
Title: Hollywood behind the lens : treasures from the Bison Archives / Marc Wanamaker and Steven Bingen.
Description: Essex, Connecticut : Lyons Press, [2024] | Includes bibliographical
references.
Identifiers: LCCN 2023043838 (print) | LCCN 2023043839 (ebook) | ISBN
9781493078554 (cloth) | ISBN 9781493085217 (epub)
Subjects: LCSH: Motion picture industry—California—Los Angeles—History. | Film
archives—United States. | Hollywood (Los Angeles, Calif.)—History. | Bison Ar-
chives—Catalogs.
Classification: LCC PN1993.42.U6 W327 2024 (print) | LCC PN1993.42.U6 (ebook)
| DDC 026.791430973—dc23/eng/20231218
LC record available at https://lccn.loc.gov/2023043838
LC ebook record available at https://lccn.loc.gov/2023043839

The paper used in this publication meets the minimum requirements of American
National Standard for Information Sciences—Permanence of Paper for Printed
Library Materials, ANSI/NISO Z39.48-1992.

CONTENTS

ACKNOWLEDGMENTS

The following individuals contributed to this book, in one way, or in many ways, either directly or inspirationally. Our deepest appreciation is owed to them.

But for now, we'll just mention their names.

Ally Acker, Richard Adkins, Marilyn Allen, the AMPAS-Margaret Herrick Library, Ann-Margret, Marie Stern Ariel, Gene Autry, Richard Bann, Ron Barbagallo, Gene Barry, John Bengston, Mary Lou Bingen, Bob Birchard, Michael F. Blake, Yvonne Blake, George Bosworth, Eddie Brandt, Kevin Brownlow, Yul Brynner, William Boyd, Hali Burton (Gail Slobodkin), the members of the band Canned Heat, Harry Carey Jr., Gil Carretero, Diana Cary, Julie Lugo Cerra, Richard Chamberlain, Charlie Chaplin, Guy Cherney, Helen Cohen, Jill Collins, Samuel Colt, Tim Considine, Anthony Coogan, Francis Ford Coppola, Mary Corliss, Ray Corrigan, Lynne Crandall, Bob Crane, Richard Crenna, Robert Cushman, Donelle Dadigan, Sharon Disney, Walt Disney, Richard Donner, James Earie, Eugene Edelman, Gary Essert, Robert Florey, James Forsher, James Franciscus, Elaina Friedrichse, Louise Gabriel, Marian Gibbons, Sam Gill, Michael Goodrow, Greg Gormick, Johnny Grant, Howard Green, Randy Haberkamp, Tom Hanlon, John Hartmann, Byron Haskin, Mike Hawks, Jill Haworth, Yascha Heifetz, Jim Heimann, Eugene Hilchey, Lena Horne, Rock Hudson, Laurie Jacobson, Marcia Jessen (www.basilrathbone.net), Fred Jordan, Richard Kaufman, Bill Kenly, Ken Kenyon, David and Rena Kiehn, Bruce Kimmel, Rob Klein, John Kobal, Richard Koszarski, Miles Kreuger, Lisa Krohn, David Ladd, Elsa Lanchester, Robert Lane, Larry Edmunds Bookshop, Larry Larson, Milt Larson, Andy Lee, Phyllis Lerner, Josef Lesser, Sol Lesser, Suzanne Lloyd and Valerie Yaros at SAG, the Los Angeles City College Theatre Arts Department, Tina Louise, Bessie Love, George Lucas, John Magruder, Mike Malone, Leonard Maltin, Howard Mandelbaum, Jeff Mantor (www.larryedmunds.com), Ernest Marquez, the Mary Pickford Foundation, Christy McAvoy, James McClosky, Col. Tim McCoy, Linda Mehr, Harold and Lillian Michelson, Clayton Moore, Movie Star News, Joseph Musso, Richard Ney, Chris Nichols, Leonard Nimoy, Donnie Norden, Fran Offenhauser, Beth Orsoff and Zoe Bingen, Jim Pauley, George Peppard, David Pierce, Stephanie Powers, Cecilia DeMille Presley, Elvis Presley, Howard Prouty, Raleigh Studios, Debbie Reynolds, Rick Rinehart, Ginger

Rogers, Roy Rogers, George and Mark Rosenthal, Margaret Ross, Anne Schlosser, Matt Severson, Rod Serling, David Shepard, Jay Silverheels, Leland Sklaar, Anthony Slide, Hylan Slobodkin, Sheila Slobodkin, Bob Smith (Howdy Doody), David Smith of the Walt Disney Archives, David Snyder, E.J. and Kimi Stephens, George Stevens Jr., Doc Stolper, Bill Stulla (Engineer Bill), Danny Swartz, Stephen X. Sylvester, Stan Taffel, Skip Taylor, Ted Tetrick, Faye Thompson, Frank Thompson, Bruce Torrence, Sophie Tucker, Martin Turnbull (www.martinturnbull.com), Wallace Umber, Mark A. Vieira, Tom Walsh, Abby, Zoe, and Jessica Wanamaker, Edith Wanamaker, Lisa Wanamaker, Sam Wanamaker, Dr. William Wanamaker, Mae West, Michael Westmore, Henry Wilcoxon, Boyd Willat, Michael Winner, Robert Wise, Rob Word, and Michael Yakaitis.

Normandie Avenue winding north into the Hollywood hills afforded 1939 motorists a breathtaking view of Griffith Observatory.

INTRODUCTION
STEVEN BINGEN

I had heard stories about Marc Wanamaker long before I met him. His name, and that of his company, Bison Archives, has long been almost as omnipotent as the phrases "Pay or play," "Thirty-Mile Zone," or "weekend grosses" within the larger Hollywood community.

When I was an archivist at Warner Bros., part of my responsibilities involved cataloging still photographs of the studio, its stars, and its library for eventual scanning, preservation, and distribution. Unfortunately, in many cases, photos that the studio held, or had once held the copyright to, no one could seem to find. The prints had been given away, or the negative had been misplaced, thrown away, lost, or misfiled. A headshot of a star, for example, could have been stored in the Feature Publicity Department, or the Television Publicity Department, or the photo lab, or with home video, or at the still archive itself, or a hundred other places. Any of which might have given away the last copy, assuming that other departments still had one, or still had a hundred on file somewhere. Therefore, it was frustrating to find a particular photograph in a book or in the TV listings in the local paper (remember those?) or in a memorabilia shop on Hollywood Boulevard, and yet the studio itself, which had created that photo, no longer had it, despite their owning it legally and—let's say this again—having produced it originally. Do you know how frustrating it is to find a photo, in print in a book, for example, with the caption "Copyright Warner Bros." on it, and yet not having a copy of it internally? Well, it is.

There was a solution to this dilemma, however. "Call Marc at Bison Archives," I was reassured by my superiors, "he'll have it."

"Marc" turned out to be the subject of this book. I called him using a number I was given from a card in my boss's Rolodex (remember those?). I started to describe the photo in question, but before I could finish, the voice on the other end of the line asked me when I needed it. There was no (very Hollywood) "let me check and we'll get back to you." No "I'll do a keyword search." And no "What studio was this at, again?" He just seemed to know off the top of his head what I wanted and that it resided in his archive, if not in ours.

The first time this happened I was working on a book that needed a photo of a 1947 strike in which picketers outside the studio had overturned a car and the police and studio security had been called in to break up the melee. Sure enough, the missing photo was rather infamous, but despite that, maybe because of that, the studio (meaning me), couldn't find a single copy of it in our files.

This was all rather odd and a little bit embarrassing. It was as if the world's largest dairy farm had to buy its own milk, one carton at a time, from a local 7-Eleven. But the transaction seemed odd to neither my superiors nor to Marc himself, who promised to send me a 4x5 negative of the photo I needed and when I needed it—which he did, and which we proceeded to use, accompanied by that "Copyright Warner Bros." designation. That photo, I might add, can now be found in this very book.

I later learned that all the studios, as well as countless other companies, used Bison to sell them back their own photos. Consequently, these organizations let him reproduce and distribute this material himself to others as well, happy that it was there if they should need it again themselves. A decidedly weird but truly symbiotic relationship, come to think of it.

Eventually, I decided that I had to meet this guy in person, which happened when he gave a presentation at Larry Edmunds Bookshop in Hollywood. Marc brought along a carousel of 35mm slides (remember those?), which he admitted to not having seen "in years," and proceeded to talk about them, masterfully, specifically, and spellbindingly, and for several hours.

A few years later I found myself working on a book of my own. One of my collaborators, Stephen X. Sylvester reassured me that Bison Archives was available to assist in the research and pictorial elements for our independent project, just as it had been for Warner Bros. and the other big guys. He was correct. Marc found us everything we needed to tell our story, and he was just as unpretentious and accessible to us during our book's genesis as he had been to me while I had the corporate might of Warner Bros. behind me. It would be the first of many fruitful collaborations between us.

I wish I could say that I know Marc Wanamaker better than I actually do, but the truth is, like his archive, there is always another wing, another shelf, another box, another document or photo or artifact shelved away awaiting discovery. I do know that there has hardly been a book about Hollywood published in recent decades that has not been enriched by his participation in it.

They say that the key to understanding a man is through his life's work. Therefore, it is my pleasure to open the doors of the Bison Archives, a collection which, like its curator, has been well-utilized in spurts and flashes in the past. But neither Marc nor his collection has ever had the opportunity to tell their own stories before. Until now.

That story, it turns out, is the story of Hollywood itself, told for the first time only through the photos and ballyhoo and ephemera that no one else had the foresight or imagination to save in one place.

The intention of this book is to turn each reader into an armchair Hollywood archivist, giving that reader the option of exploring and researching the topic of their choice amidst dozens of movieland-related subjects. It also offers those same readers a dizzying, intoxicating, kaleidoscopic ride through Hollywood history, writ large and courtesy of the very organization that first rescued and preserved so much of it for the world.

Your all-access tour of Bison Archives, with Marc Wanamaker himself as your genial host, is about to begin. Just remember that as you peruse these pages, if what you're looking for isn't here, then it probably doesn't exist any longer.

—STEVEN BINGEN
HOLLYWOOD

Marc Wanamaker as a "stunt kid" in 1955 at the erstwhile Simi Valley movie ranch and tourist attraction Corriganville.

INTRODUCTION
MARC WANAMAKER

I am a true native of Los Angeles, having been born at the Queen of Angels Hospital in Echo Park in 1947.

My father and mother, both from Chicago, came to California after World War II and settled in Los Angeles at a time when the city was recovering from both Depression and war deprivations. My father was studying to be a doctor at the time I was born. My mother had been an actress and singer from New York. Both loved the history of California and Hollywood. I also had an uncle, actor Sam Wanamaker, who had recently secured a contract with Warner Bros. in Hollywood and had starred in the film *My Girl Tisa* (1948).

In 1950, my mother began to look at houses in the hills above the Sunset Strip and east of Coldwater Canyon. She eventually found a Hollywood-style house on Beverly Crest. Constructed in 1927 in the Spanish Mission-Colonial Revival style, it had a red tiled roof, with stained glass and wrought iron details, and was situated against a hillside with its own wild forest in the rear. My mother loved the house and eventually negotiated a price for it that, while reasonable, my father could barely afford. We moved in. It is my home to this day.

Being Beverly Hills, several celebrities were already living in the neighborhood when the Wanamaker family arrived. Actors Richard Ney and Elizabeth Taylor were neighbors, as were Ethel Barrymore's son Samuel Colt, and Walt Disney's daughter Sharon. Furthermore, actors Ginger Rogers and Henry Wilcoxon and violinist Jascha Heifetz all lived a

block away on Gilcrest Drive. Other celebrities, like Charles Laughton and his wife Elsa Lanchester (both actors), became personal friends of the family.

Many of my father's patients were also in the film and television business, such as Western stars Colonel Tim McCoy, Ray "Crash" Corrigan, and Gene Barry, so it was only natural that I would gravitate toward show business. When I was about eight, I appeared in the television show *Rin Tin Tin* several times, playing the son of a Cavalry officer. Produced by ABC TV, the show was directed by famed director William Beaudine and was shot at Corrigan's ranch "Corriganville" in Simi Valley. By no small coincidence, Corrigan was a patient of my father.

Walt Disney, whose daughter, you may remember, was our neighbor, invited our family to come to the studio to see a screening of the final episode of his *Davy Crockett* series of television films, entitled *Davy Crockett and the River Pirates* (1956). After the screening, I, and a few other children there were invited to meet the show's star, Fess Parker, who presented us with our own coonskin caps as souvenirs. Walt Disney himself took a shine to me and I subsequently acted in several of his shows, such as *The Further Adventures of Spin and Marty* (1956–1957), and *Zorro* (1957–1959). The Disney people seemed to like me. I was the right age and already had experience riding a horse, thanks to some recent lessons at the Sunshine Ranch in Newhall. For some reason, despite these formative experiences, I never became a professional actor.

In the spring of 1959, I went with my family to England for the first time and lived for several months with my uncle Sam Wanamaker's family. We flew via TWA on a Constellation prop airplane, arriving in England on a cold and windy day. Back then, Heathrow Airport consisted of an open hangar that we had to walk to from our plane where the baggage and customs check-through offices were located. Sam picked us up in a car and drove us to his apartment in Regents Park.

Uncle Sam was starring in the Shakespeare play *Othello* at the new Shakespeare Memorial Theatre in nearby Stratford. He was co-starring with Paul Robeson as Othello and Mary Ure as Desdemona. During that same season, family friend Charles Laughton was working there as *King Lear,* and a young Albert Finney was also in the company. I

used to visit my uncle in his dressing room after a show, where he would be obsessing over missed lines or mistakes while still in his costume, all of which helped me to understand what an important and skilled job it is to be an actor. Maybe that's why I never became one.

We stayed in England for about five months, after which I went back home and to Emerson Jr. High, which had been built on the former site of the old Harold Lloyd studio. Upon my return, I showed my class color slides of my stay in England, and the reaction was surprisingly good despite the young age of my classmates.

In 1962, our music teacher, Mr. Umber, asked band members if we would like to appear in an upcoming film version of the hit Broadway show *The Music Man* at Warner Bros. None of us had actual marching band experience, which they said they wanted, but my friend Richard Kaufman and I were still cast in the famous "Seventy-Six Trombones" scene. We reported to the studio during school hours (Mr. Umber justified our missing school as a "learning experience"). Richard got to play one of the trombones, and I was given a set of timpani drums that had been fitted onto a two-wheeled chariot. During the shoot, my wheels intertwined with those of another chariot operated by the kid next to me. Like a scene from the film *Ben Hur*, our tangled wheels could easily have caused an accident involving stars Robert Preston and Shirley Jones, who were right in front of us. Miraculously though, this didn't happen.

In the summer of 1963, Sam Wanamaker came back to Los Angeles to appear in an episode of *The Outer Limits* television show. He played a doctor who learns that his residential neighborhood has been transported to an alien planet. The episode was entitled "A Feasibility Study," and it was shot on the old Andy Hardy Street backlot at MGM. I was allowed to visit and watch my uncle and director Byron Haskin work. Years later, in the 1970s, I interviewed Haskin for a book I was writing. He claimed to still remember me from that production.

In 1966 after graduating from high school, I enrolled at Los Angeles City College in the Music and Theater Arts departments. My father had been the school doctor there since 1954, and my mother was studying Theater Arts and Music at that time, so

it seemed preordained that I would attend there. The Theater Arts Building had just opened on the campus, and it was there that I honed my music skills and became a professional drummer. From 1967 to 1975 I played for every stage musical the Theater Arts Department produced.

An unusual event occurred during our production of *West Side Story*. At the dress rehearsal, I noticed that there were no reed players in the orchestra pit. Conductor John Magruder told me that he had been forced to fire them, as they were not up to playing such a difficult score. He assured us, though, that he had hired some replacements who were due at any minute. Sure enough, about fifteen minutes before curtain, five tall, fully bearded, long-haired men arrived, sat down, and expertly sightread through the entire show! Later I was told they were members of Frank Zappa's famed Electric Orchestra.

In 1967 I joined a group of music concert promoters. The principal founders of the new company, Kaleidoscope, were Gary Essert, John Hartmann, and Skip Taylor. Our first venue was the former Vine Street Theatre at 1228 North Vine Street in Hollywood. A round poster was designed, and the first acts to appear, April 14–16, were Jefferson Airplane, Canned Heat, and the Grateful Dead! Unfortunately, the theater owners were unhappy about having rock music performed in their venue, so they canceled our contract. In desperation, our group moved the concert to a large ballroom at the Ambassador Hotel downtown. The concert went on as scheduled to great success.

Our next show would headline The Doors and Buffalo Springfield. This time we opened at the former Ciro's nightclub on the Sunset Strip. In 1968 we changed venues again, this time to the former Earl Carroll Theatre in Hollywood, which featured the only revolving stage in Southern California. We produced several very successful shows at the theater, headlining Jefferson Airplane, The Grateful Dead, Janis Joplin, and many other popular acts.

During this time, Kaleidoscope also managed the band Canned Heat. I was assigned to be their road manager and sat in on occasion as their drummer too. We traveled together all over California, usually opening for The Grateful Dead, Jefferson Airplane, or The Doors.

In July 1968, I was recruited by a casting service to appear in the movie *Hello Dolly*, which was shooting at 20th Century Fox Studios. I was cast, again, as a member of a marching band that would parade down the studio's main street. This time I played the snare drum. It took all day to block where all the extras would be stationed and for the marching band, which was made up of smaller marching bands recruited from all over the city, to rehearse and then shoot our routine. As we were marching along, we could see the film's star, Barbra Streisand, watching us from the giant set that paralleled the parade route.

In 1969, I was asked to assist Kaleidoscope veteran Gary Essert to inaugurate the West Coast branch of the American Film Institute (AFI). To that purpose, George Stevens Jr., the organization's director, leased a Beverly Hills mansion, Greystone, as the institute's headquarters. We adapted the house, which had been built in 1929—and which, long ago, had been the site of a notorious murder-suicide—into offices, screening rooms, and other production-related facilities. My title there was "General Production Manager," but one of my first jobs was to pick up twenty-four reels of 70mm film with my Volkswagen bus and to drive it all back to the mansion, where it would be projected. The film cans filled up nearly my entire van and turned out to be a print of the Russian epic *War and Peace,* and this was to be one of its first screenings ever in the United States.

In 1970, I was tasked by AFI to take photographs of the backlots at several local studios that were either already in a state of demolition or were imminently under the threat of destruction. My first stop was MGM, the studio where I had once watched my uncle shoot that *Outer Limits* episode, and where I proceeded to shoot many photos of that same backlot's ongoing destruction by bulldozers.

I then went to Culver Studios, which had formerly been the headquarters of Thomas Ince, Cecil B. DeMille, RKO, David O. Selznick, and Lucille Ball, among others. Consequently, this lot had been where DeMille had shot *The King of Kings* (1927), where RKO had made *King Kong* (1933), and where Selznick filmed *Gone with the Wind* (1939). Most of the studio was still intact then, barely, and I shot many photos of the sets from those productions, as well as the locations for television programs such as

The Andy Griffith Show (1960–1968) and *Hogan's Heroes* (1965–1971). And I am glad I did, too, because shortly thereafter the entire backlot was demolished and developed into an industrial park.

While still working at AFI in 1971, I was appointed as a film traffic coordinator for Filmex (Los Angeles International Film Exposition), a film festival organization firm that had its offices at the Hollywood Roosevelt Hotel and often screened their movies across the street at Grauman's Chinese Theatre.

In March of that year, I took time off from both my duties at AFI and at Filmex to travel to Spain to work as a fourth assistant director on the motion picture *Catlow*, directed by Sam Wanamaker and starring Yul Brynner, Leonard Nimoy, and Richard Crenna. I spent several weeks working on the film and then traveled all over Europe in a Volkswagen camper. I finally ended up in London, where I stayed with my uncle.

On my return to Hollywood, I enrolled in the Theater Arts program at a San Fernando Valley state college known, aptly, as "Valley State." While there I was involved in several plays and musicals, working on various jobs, such as costume designer and as a director. I was at Valley State for two years, culminating in a bachelor's degree in theater.

Back at AFI, I helped to set up a library on the history of the motion picture industry. I was doing this on a fateful day when I took a call from a woman who told me that she was a senior publicist at Columbia Studios. She was inquiring as to the possibility of donating their entire still photograph collection. At the time, Columbia was moving from its longtime home on Gower Street in Hollywood, and her bosses had told her to leave the collection behind. I checked with George Stevens Jr., who assigned me to arrange the donation, transport it all to Greystone, and then catalog the entire collection. At the time, none of us could have foreseen how big a job this was going to be. It ended up taking two years.

As I explored the collection, I was shocked to discover that I'd never heard of many of the film titles on the stills. How could that be? It turned out that these photos had been filed according to a film's working title, which often would turn out to not necessarily be the same name that the films had ultimately been released under. Someone suggested

that I go to the Academy of Motion Picture Arts and Sciences to try to discover what the final release titles had been for Columbia Pictures' entire library. Today there are books and websites answering these questions, but at the time the Academy was the only place with the answers. Needless to say, I ended up spending a *lot* of time over there. I didn't know it then, but in 1973 Filmex would move their offices to donated space at, ironically, the old Columbia Studios lot on Gower, whose photo library I had been laboriously indexing. So eventually, I would spend a *lot* of time working over there as well.

In my ongoing quest to unlock the secrets of the Columbia Library, I started perusing industry newsletters, books, and periodicals such as *The Film Daily Yearbook, Moving Picture World,* and *Motion Picture News.* I became fascinated with the wider history of other American film companies as well. As I researched Columbia Pictures, I sadly realized that the other studios' history was falling through the cracks as well. It shocked me that no one had ever published an encyclopedic reference on American motion picture studios.

Starting in 1972, I embarked on researching this dream project. The Academy of Motion Picture Arts and Sciences, where I had started out, continued to be a primary resource for photographs and source materials, but I widened my research from there and found many other resources in the Los Angeles area for such materials. These included Larry Edmunds Bookshop in Hollywood, which opened in 1938 and was, and is, a treasure-trove of film studio-related materials. Other resources where I found photographs and collectibles included Eddie Brandt's Saturday Matinee, Collectors Bookshop, Cherokee Bookshop, Ray Stuart Photo Archives, Bennett's Book Store, Bond Street Book Store, H&H Book Store, The Scroungers, Hollywood Book and Poster, Star World, Movie World, American Stock Photos, First American Title Insurance Archives, First Federal Savings and Loan of Hollywood, Henry Huntington Library, Dick Whittington Stock Photo, Los Angeles Public Library Photographic Archive, UCLA Theatre Arts Library, UCLA Spence aerial photo collection, and Acres of Books in Long Beach.

My book project got bigger and bigger as I found more and more material to include. Eventually, I traveled to New York and would return every year for twenty years to

access materials from Cinemabilia, Movie Star News, Mark Ricci's Memory Shop, Jerry Ohlinger's Movie Materials Store, the New York Public Library, the City Museum of New York, Lincoln Center Archives, and the Museum of Modern Art Photographic Archives, among others. If asked to estimate, I'd guess that about a third of the eventual Bison Archives core materials were originally sourced out of New York.

Yet this still was not enough! My research trips became international. I went to London and explored the collections of The Cinema Bookshop, Better Books, Samuel French Theatre Bookshop, Motely Books, and the British Film Institute's photographic archive. In France, the Cinematheque Francoise photographic library was a wonderful resource for studio images as well.

The list of places where I found and then preserved valuable materials from was endless. No one else, except for a few private individuals, seemed to be seriously collecting these materials at the time. And sadly, those that were collecting on this subject seemed to delight in not sharing what they had found with anyone else! As my collection grew, and grew, I was encouraged by my friends and colleagues to create not just a book but my own archive. A specifically cinema-related archive that would then be available to other researchers, to authors, to historians, and to the entertainment industry itself.

So, I did. I named it Bison Archives after the second film company to come to California in 1909, The Bison Film Company. It seems that I had set out to create a book and had ended up creating a company.

An invaluable resource for that company turned out to be the various studios' internal research libraries. All the majors had carefully maintained these libraries for decades, but in the 1970s these collections were being marginalized, closed, limited in their work, or sold off outright from within.

I went to these libraries and found part-time work, and lifetime friends there. My bosses James Earie of MGM, Kellem DeForest of RKO-Paramount, Andy Lee of Universal, and Ken Kenyon of 20th Century Fox realized what was in danger of happening to their libraries and helped me to acquire their pertinent, cinema-related materials, including books, magazines, clipping files, photographs, and other memorabilia, much of

which I would preserve for them and eventually donate to the Academy of Motion Picture Arts and Sciences Library. These invaluable, priceless internal studio materials eventually would make up another third of Bison Archives' holdings.

The result of all this hoarding and collecting was that Bison Archives would become a world-class specialty archive devoted to the history of the motion picture, television, and radio industries and a Los Angeles–centric regional archive on the history of California and its connection to the entertainment industry. As such, I am very proud to say that Bison Archives has now contributed to hundreds of books, magazines, newspapers, websites, and all other media types from around the world related to the entertainment industry.

Just as a representative sampling, some of the books that I have either written myself or collaborated with colleagues on include *Star Profiles, Reel Women, Hollywood Haunted, Destined for Hollywood, Hollywood Past and Present, Los Angeles Past and Present, Early Beverly Hills, Beverly Hills 1940–2008, Early Hollywood, Hollywood 1940–2008, Theatres in Los Angeles, Westwood, Early Warner Bros. Studios, Location Filming in Los Angeles, Griffith Park, San Fernando Valley, Movie Studios of Culver City, Early Paramount Studios, Early Poverty Row Studios, Max Factor and Hollywood, Paramount City of Dreams, The Cochranes and the Founding of Universal Pictures, Hollywood's Lost Backlot,* and *Hollywood Trains and Trolleys.*

Bison Archives has also become, somewhat ironically, suppliers and consultants for the studios themselves. As such, I have contributed photos and historic research for their in-house newsletters, articles, displays, and publicity releases. I've also been tasked by the studios to help create or improve upon their studio tours and have worked with various departments regarding the history and usage of their physical lots.

I have continued to work in film production myself as well. In 1974, I was working for director Michael Winner and came up with the idea of a film about how Rin Tin Tin (the dog star, and my one-time costar) had saved Warner Bros. from financial ruin in the 1920s. Later, in 1976, Winner produced and directed a film titled *Won Ton Ton: The Dog Who Saved Hollywood,* a comedy based on my story outline.

13

An interesting and consistent function of Bison Archives over the years has been as a technical advisor on feature films. This started in 1975 when the Art Department for Paramount's *The Day of the Locust* approached me for historical photographs of Grauman's Chinese Theatre, which they would then use to build a replica of. After this job, other art directors and production designers began to use Bison Archives, and me, for their own (usually) Hollywood-set projects as well. The feature films I have contributed to include *Hearts of the West* (1975), *Nickelodeon* (1976), *Gable and Lombard* (1976), *1941* (1979), *Mommie Dearest* (1981), *Frances* (1982), *Blade Runner* (1982), *My Favorite Year* (1982), *Streets of Fire* (1984), *The Woman in Red* (1984), *Sunset* (1988), *The Two Jakes* (1990), *The Doors* (1991), *Bram Stoker's Dracula* (1992), *L.A. Confidential* (1997), *The Aviator* (2004), *Hollywoodland* (2006), *Gangster Squad* (2016), *Hail Caesar!* (2016), and *Once Upon a Time in Hollywood* (2019).

Documentaries and television productions have been consistent Bison Archive clients. Projects to which I have contributed in this capacity include *Hollywood: The Pioneers* (1979–80), *Charlie Chaplin: The Little Tramp* (1980), *Buster Keaton* (1981), *Ticket to Hollywood* (1983), *Unknown Chaplin* (1983), *The Making of a Legend: Gone With the Wind* (1988), *The Universal Story* (1996), *Frank Capra's American Dream* (1997), *True Hollywood Story* (1997), *Glorious Technicolor* (1998), *American Experience* (1999), *Hollywood Moguls* (2000), *Hearst Castle* (2000), *Edith Head* (2000), *The Lot* (2000), *The Men Who Made the Movies* (2002), *The Desilu Story* (2003), *I Am King Kong* (2005), *Garbo: Biography* (2005), *Beverly Hilton Hotel* (2014), *Be Natural* (2016), and *Walt Disney* (2016).

Since the 1970s, I have been affiliated with many Hollywood-related museums and societies, including the Academy of Motion Picture Arts and Sciences, the American Film Institute, and the Natural History Museum of Los Angeles County. I am also a co-founder or contributor to the Beverly Hills Historical Society, Santa Monica Historical Museum, the Autry Museum of the American West, the Culver City Historical Society, and the Venice Historical Society.

A thirty-year (and counting) relationship with another such organization began inadvertently when I was on a research expedition at Paramount Studios. In a corner of their

western town set then stood an old barn that had been used by Cecil B. DeMille when he had made his first film, *The Squaw Man* in 1913. I never would have guessed then how important that old barn would turn out to be in my life. Built in 1901, this structure had originally stood on the corner of Selma and Vine Streets and had been moved to the studio lot in 1926. But by 1980, the barn had been moved off-lot again, and it was only through the intervention of a then-new preservation organization, Hollywood Heritage, that the structure survived and was eventually designated as their permanent home. Over the years I have donated many historic artifacts to their museum located inside that barn, and I continue to be involved with programming and exhibits there.

After all these years, my encyclopedia of American film studios is still very much a work in progress. That said, hundreds of other books, by myself and others, have already benefited from its long genesis.

That's a pretty good legacy.

—MARC WANAMAKER
BISON ARCHIVES

Bison Archives' official logo, based on the Bison Film Company insignia of 1919.

Marc Wanamaker in 1952, holding, naturally enough, a movie camera.

Marc joins the cavalry for a Rin Tin Tin *episode, 1954.*

On the road (well, Beverly Glen) with the band Canned Heat, 1969.

All the studios once maintained vast research libraries that contained the sum totals of worldwide human knowledge on every subject imaginable. Marc diligently researching at 20th Century Fox in 1975.

chapter 1

THE PIONEERS AND THE SCALAWAGS

ORIGINS, LEGENDS, CON MEN, AND LIES

The name "Hollywood" is as mysterious and illusive and contradictory as the product it creates. Holly is a well-known flowering plant of which there are over five-hundred varieties—none of which are to be found naturally in southern California, and most of which are classified by botanists as shrubs, which means that the majority of holly plants do not themselves produce wood.

So, the name "Holly-wood" is a lie. This is appropriate, though, because the film industry is itself built upon deception, exaggeration, optical tricks, and a suspension of disbelief.

Starting around 1887 when the name "Hollywood" was first used on a parcel map to refer to the property, Kansas real estate developer Harvey H. Wilcox and his second wife, Daeida, along with two businessmen, H.J. Whitley and Charles E. Toberman, began variously purchasing, developing, and dividing assorted properties north of what was then the city of Los Angeles.

Harvey and Daeida are usually characterized as being strict prohibitionists. Although there is little actual evidence that this is the case, the ironic sting inherent in imagining that the community that would later foster such colorful alcoholics as John Barrymore, W.C. Fields, Raymond Chandler, Errol Flynn, and Charles Bukowski was founded by two teetotalers is just too good not to be repeated here. Unquestionably, the Wilcoxes were a civic-minded couple; they eventually donated the land for three local churches in the neighborhood. So, it is probably true that the (then) disreputable entertainment industry—although, of course, it would not have been called that yet—was among the last business that they would have welcomed into their little city.

Incidentally, at least six other states also can boast of communities with the name "Hollywood," most of which are older than, encompass more real estate than, or have populations larger than the California edition.

Hollywood, California was incorporated as a city in 1903, but was annexed into greater Los Angeles in 1910 to take advantage of the larger nearby city's water supply, which was in the process of being secured through events that would eventually be fictionalized into one of the greatest of all Los Angeles movies, *Chinatown* (1974).

How the movies came to Hollywood is also in dispute. Once upon a time, long, long ago, legendary director Cecil B. DeMille appeared on a talk show in the twilight of his remarkable career and was asked if he had been influenced by earlier filmmakers. As if the question itself was impertinent and inane, there was a slight pause before the great man deemed to answer it at all, saying, "There were no earlier filmmakers."

That statement, grandiose as it is, is not quite accurate, of course. DeMille, if not the first filmmaker in Hollywood, was the first to realize that, like Hollywood itself, the entertainment industry needed an origin story, a place to come from, and a person, or a people, to stand in the resultant limelight and to take a bow.

That bow could have been taken in New Jersey, or England, or France or any of a dozen other places where movies were "invented," or produced or exhibited, near the end of the nineteenth century. We do know that DeMille, at the bequest of his partners, Samuel Goldwyn, Jesse Lasky, and Adolph Zukor, went west to California to make a movie in 1913. The variety of cheap locations, unenforced patent laws, and unlimited sunshine that California offered kept them there. But Hollywood, where DeMille and company eventually ended up, was only one of several filmmaking outposts that were bubbling up then all over neighborhoods in Southern California and elsewhere.

Hollywood itself, however, was central to most of these early "studios." It still is. The so-called "Thirty-Mile Zone" (TMZ) that labor unions officially designate as "Hollywood" for the purposes of determining workers' compensation is a tangible illustration of this. It is probable that the name "Hollywood" became attached to that industry as well as to a specific place just because that name was, as the Wilcoxes discovered, evocative, and yet then still relatively nonspecific, even generic. So, like other (originally) unremarkable names—John Wayne, Charlie Brown, Jonestown, Wall Street, Atlantic City, and Woodstock, among others—it takes on personality and dimension only because of how it is used and who it is used by.

Cecil B. DeMille and his contemporaries, and his followers and successors were, far from being the creative, artistic dreamers and schemers they are now depicted as, nobly working to forge a new art and a new industry with rolled up sleeves and jodhpurs. Instead, these "pioneers" were more akin to the carpetbaggers who descended upon the South after the Civil War. But like the carpetbaggers, some of them anyway, they eventually learned to love that which would have initially been only a financial opportunity. Hollywood's early moguls, at least the best of them eventually, perhaps unconsciously, discovered that they liked the movies, almost as much as they liked the financial rewards that these movies could bring.

Built in 1892 in West Orange, New Jersey, Thomas Edison's "Black Maria" was the first purpose-built motion picture studio in the world.

One of the first motion pictures to be publicly exhibited, ever, was Edison's The Kiss *(1896).*

That said, the idea of titling a film at all had not yet been officially conceived of, so that moniker was apparently used only later to identify the subject of this eighteen-second epic—which climaxes with a smooch between pictured lovebirds Mary Irwin and John Rice. It is worth noting though, that even at this early point, stage actors and adaptations (Irwin and Rice were recreating a scene from their play, The Widow Jones*) were already being highlighted, along with a dose of sex, of course.*

Farragut Theatre
TO-NIGHT
EDISON'S PROJECTOSCOPE
The 19th Century Marvel.

—AMONG THE VIEWS TO BE SHOWN—

Village Blacksmith
Portion of the Procession attending the Ceremonies at the Coronation of the Czar of Russia at Moscow
Loading a Coke Oven at Carmaux, France
March of the French African Soldiers
Juggler Trewry in his famous Ribbon Act
Arrival of Family
Aquarium
German Dragoons.
Hurdle Jumping.

Spanish Artillery
Chicago Police Parade
Tearing down an old Building
Street Dances, London
Whirlpool Rapids
Arrival of Fast Mail, Paris
Spanish Infantry
Game of Cards
Children at Play.
Gardner and Bad Boy
Quarreling Babies
Caravan of Camels, Egypt
Street in Cario
St. Marc, Venice
Russian Dance, Etc

Edison's wonderful Projectoscope will be seen at the Farragut Theatre one night only, Wednesday December 8th. This machine is without a doubt the best and most perfect ever shown to the public. Next to life itself nothing is so real as the Projectoscope. It reproduces nature and natural movements with such resemblance that confound the spectators who are obliged to believe that it is life itself that is before their eyes.

Special Low Prices; 15 cts, 25 cts and 35 cts
SEATS NOW ON SALE AT HARRIER & SON'S.
VALLEJO CHRONICLE PRINT.

A HANDBILL OF AN ITINERANT EXHIBITOR OF 1897

Many of the earliest films were single-shot travelogues and tableaux depicting such thrilling spectacles as quarreling babies and a village blacksmith plying his trade, which must have astonished nineteenth-century audiences (1897 ad).

EDISON FILMS

PATENTED AND COPYRIGHTED.

Replete with Thrilling and Exciting Incidents in Fourteen Scenes,

THE GREAT TRAIN ROBBERY

Was shown to enthusiastic houses during Xmas week in New York at the following theatres :

**Hurtig & Seamon's
Circle Theatre
Proctor's 125th St.**

**SEND FOR FULLY
ILLUSTRATED
AND
DESCRIPTIVE
PAMPHLET.**

**Keith's 14th St.
Harlem Opera House
Tony Pastor's
Eden Musee
Huber's Museum
Orpheum, Brooklyn
Comedy Theatre
Orpheum Music Hall**

**LENGTH, 740
FEET.
PRICE, $111.
CODE WORD,
VACUNABAN.**

Edison Exhibition Kinetoscope, $115.00. Edison Universal Kinetoscope, $75.00.

MAIN OFFICE and FACTORY, Orange, N. J.

EDISON MANUFACTURING CO., NEW YORK OFFICE: 83 Chambers St.

OFFICE FOR UNITED KINGDOM : 52 Gray's Inn Road, Holborn, London, W.C., England.
EUROPEAN OFFICE : 32 Rempart Saint Georges, Antwerp, Belg

SELLING AGENTS:

THE KINETOGRAPH CO.................................41 E. 21st St., New York
KLEINE OPTICAL CO.................................52 State St., Chicago, Ill.
PETER BACIGALUPI.................................933 Market St., San Francisco, Cal.

THE ORIGINAL AND ONLY

As one of the first narrative films to use modern cinematic effects, Edison's twelve-minute The Great Train Robbery (1903) has a lot to answer for. It was also, in its time, so hugely successful with audiences around the world that several shot-for-shot remakes were allegedly produced by others. Note the "original and only" designation in this trade ad.

Several historians have referred to the actor pictured here as future Western star G.M. "Bronco Billy" Anderson. It isn't. Instead, it was Justus D. "George" Barnes, who in the film, as here, shocked audiences by firing his pistol right at them.

The performer in this 1905 Biograph peep show comedy is unknown, although she undoubtedly attracted her fair share of admirers.

Harvey and Daeida Wilcox were two of the founders of Hollywood, although they probably would not have been pleased with how things worked out there (1887 photos).

Harvey Wilcox's 1887 colorful and somewhat fanciful tract map of "Beautiful Hollywood" also, rather improbably, includes Santa Monica and pictures the future Hollywood Hills upsized to nearly Biblical proportions. Likewise, it should be noted that the "Hotel Hollywood" seen here was never built as such—and should not be confused with the later "Hollywood Hotel," which was.

Above, in 1895 a group of lonely children posed for a photographer in the middle of Western Avenue, which intersects with Sunset Boulevard behind them. Below, the same intersection, more or less, in 2023.

Prospect Avenue looking east to the intersection of Highland Avenue in 1905; five years later the former street would be renamed Holly-wood Boulevard.

In 1896, William Selig founded a company that bore his name. In 1909, he built the first permanent movie studio in Los Angeles, in Edendale, seen here in 1913.

Looking south down North Orange Drive in 1910, an early tourist would have seen the newly renamed Hollywood Boulevard running east to west. The large house with the little tower in the foreground would be purchased by the American Society of Cinematographers in 1936 and remains their clubhouse to this day.

Bison Film Company, which specialized in westerns, was the second film company to come to California. In this 1910 photo they celebrate their first anniversary.

It may not look like much, but in 1911 the Nester Motion Picture Company, built the first motion picture studio in Hollywood, on the northwest corner of Sunset and Gower. In 1912, Nester would merge with Universal (1911 photo).

Vitagraph Studios, located at 1415 Ocean Avenue in Santa Monica, opened in 1911. They later moved to East Hollywood (Las Feliz) before being purchased by Warner Bros. in 1925 (1912 photo).

A 1913 exhibitors survey of film production studio logos. Although some of the companies listed here would eventually mutate/survive into the twenty-first century, note that none of them were yet based in any place called "Hollywood."

"Director General" Cecil B. DeMille (seated, and already wearing his trademark boots) with the cast and crew of The Squaw Man, *the first significant feature film made in Hollywood, California (1913 photo).*

Producer Jesse Lasky at the barn location on Selma and Vine where DeMille made The Squaw Man, *and made history and which led to the creation of Paramount Pictures (1919 photo).*

Keystone's Mack Sennett directs cameraman Hans F. Koenekamp and cast on the set of Stolen Magic *(1915).*

Pioneer Hollywood still photographer Nelson Evans is thought to have taken this charming portrait of assorted aspiring Christie, Universal, and Sennett starlets, circa 1916.

The Fine Arts Studio at 4500 Sunset Boulevard in East Hollywood as it looked in 1915, the year D.W. Griffith made his landmark epic The Birth of a Nation *there and transformed the movies from a gimmick to an art form.*

Babylon, as visualized in Griffith's Intolerance *(1916), contained one of the largest sets ever built for a motion picture.*

Griffith's Babylon sets hauntingly continued to stand at Fine Arts Studio for several years after their construction (1916–1919 photos).

A stylized copy of Intolerance*'s Babylon was completed in 2001 at the Hollywood & Highland Center, some two and a half miles from where the original had stood (2010 photo).*

Thomas Ince, seen here in 1915, was a creative early producer who was responsible for many of the innovations that made it possible to create films in a factory setting.

Inceville Light House Moving Picture Village by the Sea,
Southern California.

Ince's studio, "Inceville," was built on the beach in Pacific Palisades, which made realistic pictorial compositions such as this one possible (1916 postcard).

Harry Houdini, the master of escape, and his young and pretty wife, were visitors to Inceville this week. The noted performer, who has startled the world by his

Harry Houdini, master of escape, turning an Inceville camera under the direction of Scott Sidney.

feats of skill, was escorted about the plant by Producer Ince and marveled at the many wonders unfolded before him.

Legendary magician Harry Houdini, who worked intermittently in the movies between 1918 and 1923, here pays a visit to Inceville with his wife, Bess, and director Scott Sidney (1919 article).

Inceville continued to be used as a studio until 1922, although some of the structures there, abandoned, vandalized, and gutted by fire, stood on the site for several years after that. This Auto Club road sign, however, curiously dates from 1930, several years after the studio itself was only a haunted memory.

MERIT FILM CORPORATION

206 FILM EXCHANGE BUILDING

MINNEAPOLIS, MINN.

Feb. 20, 1922 ....192......

Mr. David Horsley,
725-7th Ave,
New York City, N.Y.

Dear Mr. Horsley:

     I have your favor of the 16th quoting prices
on various product. While I realize that there is more
money to be made in the outright purchase of film, conditions
in this market at the present time are such that we are
positively not investing any money in outside product and
would much prefer to play these pictures on a 50/50 basis.

     Shall be very glad to hear from you.

        Yours very truly,

        MERIT FEDERATED FILM CO.

        Manager.

AW*LF

In 1913 producer William Selig opened a zoo that also served film productions in need of exotic animals. Future mogul Louis B. Mayer opened his first studio on the site and the Warner Brothers took early advantage of the location and its furry performers (1922 correspondence).

chapter 2

SILENT LOVERS AND SAD CLOWNS

HOLLYWOOD'S EARLY BOOM TOWN DAYS, AND NIGHTS

The American cinema star system was born in 1910 when an actress named Florence Lawrence became famous specifically for appearing in films, eventually leading her producer, Carl Laemmle, to realize that audiences would patronize those films because she appeared in them.

From these auspicious beginnings, the star system became the most important cog in a studio's vast assembly line. Big stars could be counted on to enhance a picture's expected box office take solely on the strength of those stars' appeal. The stars, of course, realized this and were able to command enormous salaries. Charlie Chaplin, for example, was paid $1 million in 1918 for his services (albeit in eight films), reportedly the first time in history a human being was paid a salary that high for anything.

Stars were, and are, not the only way to attract patronage from audiences. The studios, and those audiences too, quickly discovered the appeal of movies with recognizable and well-liked settings, characters, or situations. Comedies and westerns were among the first genres to be embraced by movies—and by movie audiences. As odd as it seems today, supernatural horror stories, and stories derived from comic books, now wildly popular, were initially only produced as low-budget, or juvenile fodder, if at all.

Silent star Lillian Gish once said that talkies should have evolved into silent movies instead of the other way around. Some might disagree, although there is no denying that by the late 1920s there was no action, emotion, mood, or comic or dramatic device that could not be conveyed by the silent camera, and by silent stars, to audiences.

Mary Pickford was twenty-five and married when she played the eleven-year-old title role in Poor Little Rich Girl, *but her fans would not have had it any other way, and she would continue to convincingly play teenagers and adolescents for another decade. Here she is flanked by her director, Maurice Tourneur, and cameraman Lucien Andriot (1917 photo).*

Mary Pickford was one of the most popular actresses of her time — of all time — and Paramount was obviously delighted to have her exclusively from 1914 to 1916.

During the silent era, theater owners would often project glass, hand-tinted slides touting both their future attractions and local businesses, and their studio would then print ads rhapsodizing about the box office results. One wonders if S.A. Stevens & Son were as happy with those results as United Artists was with Douglas Fairbanks' successful star turn as Robin Hood *(1922).*

Mary Pickford and Douglas Fairbanks clown around. The couple married in 1920 to a rapturous public response that arguably has not been matched by any celebrity hookup since. The supercouple divorced in 1936, and when he died three years later Pickford was reportedly inconsolable.

Just before becoming one of the most popular men of the twentieth century and the single-most important individual in Hollywood history, Charlie Chaplin here looks almost impossibly vulnerable and (thanks in part to colorization) contemporary, at the age of twenty-seven. He had just signed a contract with Mutual Film that would make him one of the highest-paid people up until that time (1916 photo).

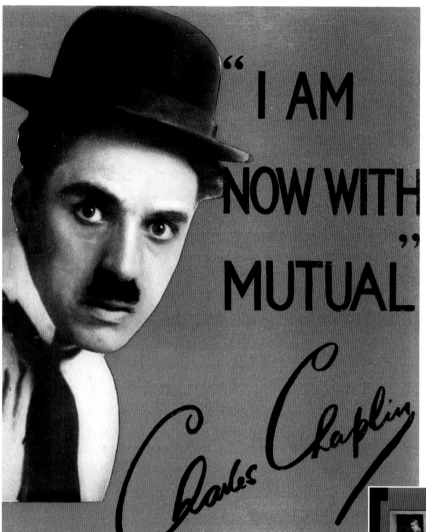

"I AM NOW WITH" MUTUAL

Charles Chaplin

Mutual Film would make the most of their very expensive but ultimately lucrative deal with Charlie Chaplin, who would go on to even greater fame — and compensation — elsewhere, but the company itself would ultimately be absorbed by RKO (1916 trade ads).

CHARLES CHAPLIN & JOHN R. FREULER SIGNING CONTRACT

Statement by Charles Chaplin

AFTER thoroughly investigating the motion picture field, I have decided to affiliate myself with the **MUTUAL FILM CORPORATION**. My future pictures will be released by Mutual exchanges because they serve the greatest number of exhibitors throughout the country.

Mutually yours,
CHARLES CHAPLIN.

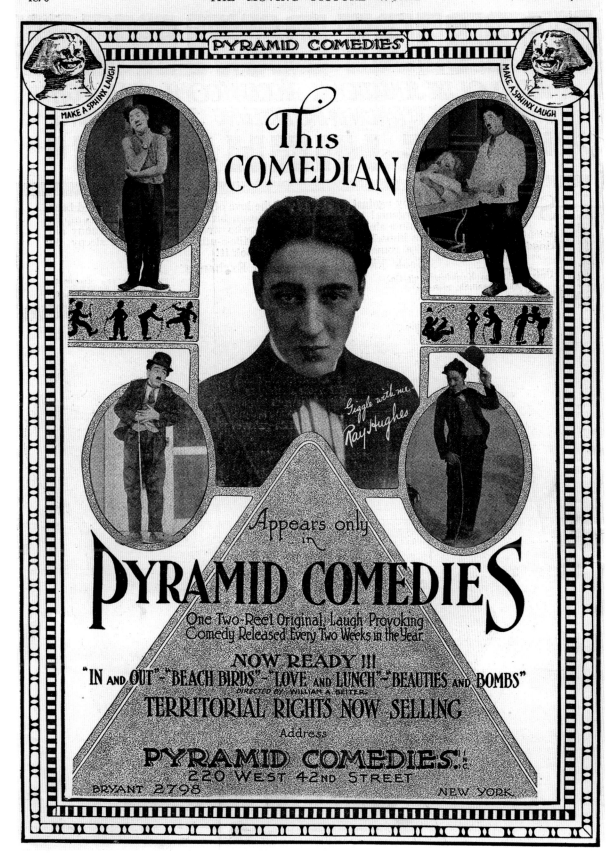

Charlie Chaplin never worked for "Pyramid Comedies," but it's difficult indeed to ascertain that fact from this cheeky 1917 trade ad.

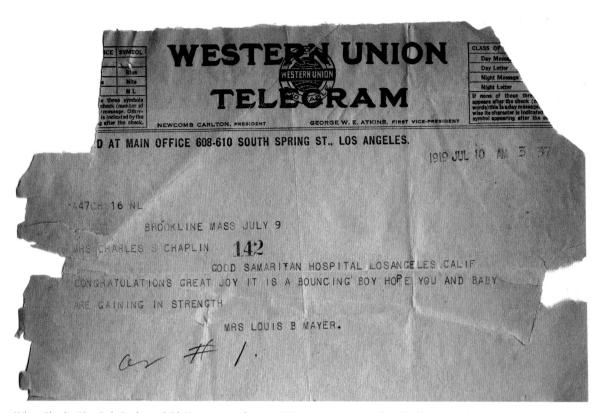

When Charlie Chaplin's firstborn child, Norman, was born in 1919, Margaret Mayer, the wife of then aspiring mogul Louis B. Mayer, sent this congratulatory telegram. Tragically, Norman would die the day after this message arrived.

Charlie Chaplin once said, "All I need to make a comedy are a park bench, a cop, and a pretty girl." The pretty girl (Edna Purviance, in this film) is missing here, but Sunset Park in Beverly Hills still makes for a pretty backdrop for The Idle Class (1921 photo).

Charlie Chaplin was one of the first celebrities to be heavily merchandised. Here Photoplay *magazine gets into the act by offering its readers cut-out paper dolls featuring costumes and canines and an attachable mustache from some of his then-current comedies (1919 layout).*

Fans outside the Liberty Theatre in Bellingham, Washington compete in a Charlie Chaplin lookalike contest in this 1921 photo. According to legend, Chaplin himself once entered such a contest, and came in twentieth!

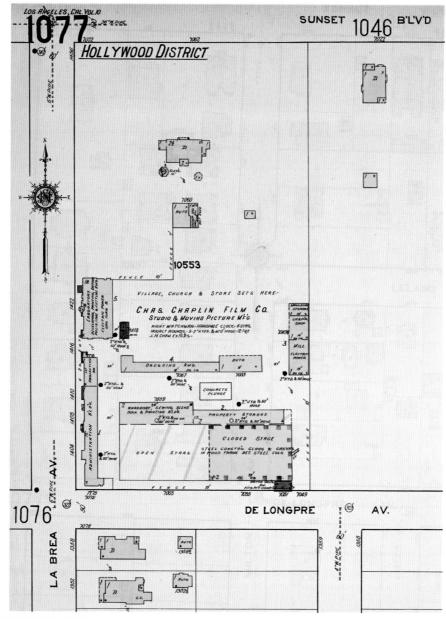

HOLLYWOOD DISTRICT

10553

VILLAGE, CHURCH & STORE SETS HERE·

CHAS. CHAPLIN FILM CO.
STUDIO & MOVING PICTURE MF'G.

NIGHT WATCHMAN - HARDINGE CLOCK - 6 STRS.
HOURLY ROUNDS - 3 - 2" H'YDS. & 400' HOSE - 12 1 QT.
J.H. CHEM. EXTG'RS·

ELECTRIC POWER

LABORATORY
DEVELOPING, DRYING,
PRINTING, POLISHING &
CUTTING RMS.

MOULDING STORAGE
CHAPL. SHOP
MILL
ELECTRIC POWER

DRESSING RMS.
AUTO

PROJECTING BL'DG.

CONCRETE PLUNGE

ADMINISTRATION BL'DG.

HARDROBE, SEWING, SCENE
DOCK & PAINTING BL'DG.

PROPERTY STORAGE

CLOSED STAGE
STEEL CONSTR'N. GLASS & CANVAS
IN WOOD FRAME BET. STEEL COLS.

OPEN STAGE

1076

LA BREA AV.

DE LONGPRE AV.

AUTO
AUTO

Chaplin maintained his own studio at 1416 North La Brea Avenue, the design of which well-reflected his British roots. The lot is seen here as represented by a Sanborn Fire Insurance map from 1919, as it looked in 1921, 1938, 1953 (during its tenure as A&M Records), and in 2023 as the current home of Jim Henson Productions. Look closely at the very last image, however; it is a replica of the studio, built in Filmore, California for the 1992 biographical film Chaplin.

Best friends Charlie Chaplin and Douglas Fairbanks clown together at a well-attended Liberty Loan drive in New York City in August 1918.

Buster Keaton, seen here in The General, *was, artistically, if not financially, Chaplin's only serious rival as silent cinema's greatest clown (1927 photo).*

Buster Keaton, far right, in front of his studio at Lillian Way and Eleanor Avenue, with his sister Louise, mother Myra, and brother Harry, who was professionally known as "Jingles" (circa 1924 photo).

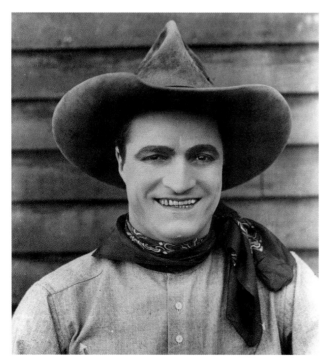

Tom Mix and William S. Hart were both born in the East and both became famous playing cowboys, although Hart's westerns were as gritty and realistic as Mix's were fanciful and fun (circa 1920 photos).

Lon Chaney, one of the most fascinating and enigmatic personalities of his era, shows off his legendary makeup box and his legendary makeup for The Phantom of the Opera *(1925). Fortunately, the makeup kit survives and is now part of the permanent collection of the Natural History Museum of Los Angeles County.*

Cecil B. DeMille (far left) at Paramount directing Fool's Paradise. *Things had already changed since 1913, however. Here he is assisted by editor Anne Bauchens and by Karl Struss and Alvin Wyckoff, manning cameras (1921 photo).*

For DeMille's 1923 version of The Ten Commandments, *twenty-one sphinxes such as this and a 100-foot-tall "Gate of Rameses" were constructed at the Guadalupe Sand Dunes in Santa Barbara County, California. When the film was completed, the sets were buried and abandoned, where they remain today, possibly awaiting speculation by future archeologists as to when the ancient Egyptians settled North America.*

Erich Von Stroheim, seen here at Universal in 1923, was one of the era's most creative, obsessive, and ultimately self-destructive talents. By the 1930s he was no longer able to secure financing to direct his own productions and thereafter mostly worked as an actor, often parodying his own Prussian, autocratic persona.

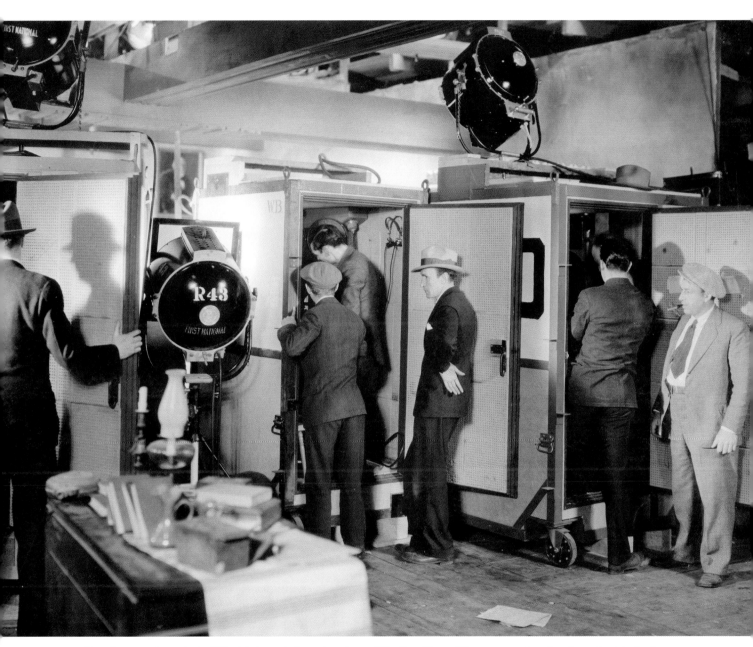

Sound came to the movies in 1927 with the explosive, noisy release of The Jazz Singer. *The camera made such a clatter that it had to be packed in airless soundproof boxes, as seen here at Warner Bros. (1929 photo).*

Crowds lined up for Mary Pickford's first talkie, Coquette, *and her performance would win her an Academy Award. But the film would also be the beginning of the end of her reign as America's sweetheart and of an era in history (1929 photo).*

chapter 3

EMPERORS AND EMPIRES

THE STUDIOS, FROM THE MAJORS TO POVERTY ROW, FROM FRONT OFFICES TO BACKLOTS

ather romantically, the major studios that constitute corporate Hollywood have long been collectively referred to as "The Seven Sisters," a name ripe with evocative echoes of Greek myth and familial collectiveness. Although it's true that there have, since the beginning, been seven powerful studios largely determining what the American film industry will turn its cameras toward, it has not always been the *same* seven studios. For example, RKO's last days as a major in the late 1950s coincide almost exactly with Disney's ascent into the big time.

During Hollywood's "golden era," however, it was another—more accurate if less evocative—name that was usually used in the industry to define its most powerful entities, "the big five." The big five were MGM, Paramount, Warner Bros.,

20th Century Fox, and RKO. Nipping at their heels, there were also what was then known as the "little three": Universal, Columbia, and United Artists.

Today, Fox is owned by Disney, and United Artists by MGM, which is owned by Amazon, and which itself is now only accorded the status of "mini-major" in the Hollywood firmament, leaving—again—five vertically integrated companies in control of everything.

Not quite everything. There were, then and now, also several important independent studios, and several not so important but still interesting smaller outfits that did, and do, compete with the majors for market share and audience favor.

Let's take a look, through photographs, maps, and documents, at the seven sisters, the big five, the little three, and the indies.

Paramount Pictures wasn't the first Los Angeles–based studio that survives today (Universal was also founded in 1912). But the construction of Paramount's iconic gate in 1926 feels like an organic place to begin a photo survey of Hollywood factories. That same gate survives today as both a beacon and as a barrier to aspiring movie stars and technicians from across the decades (1926 and 2010 photos).

For its 1928 version of Gentlemen Prefer Blondes, *the Paramount Gate was besieged by actual and potential blondes looking to be cast in the film.*

**ORDERS TAKEN
FOR HOMEMADE
PIES TO TAKE OUT
50c EACH**

**Paramount
Studio Cafe**

**FOUNTAIN SERVICE
UNTIL 5:30 P. M.**

RELISHES AND APPETIZERS
Hearts of Celery 20   Celery a la Victor 35
Stuffed Celery with Roquefort Cheese 35
Sweet or Dill Pickles 15
Anchovies Canape 45
Imported Beluga Caviar Canape 45
Can of Imported Sardines 50

COCKTAILS SUPREME
SERVED IN ICE
Lobster 35   Crab Meat 35   Avocado 30
Louisiana Prawns 35   California Fruit 35
Combination Melon Balls 35
Combination Seafood 25   Tomato Juice 15
Sauerkraut Juice 15   Eastern Clam Juice 15

SOUPS
Special Cream of Fresh Mushroom,
au Terraine 30
Creamed Oyster Stew 30
Consomme Florentine 20
Chicken Gumbo Creole with Rice 10

SEAFOOD IN SEASON
Breaded Filet of Frisco Sole,
Sauce Tartar, Cole Slaw 50
Fresh Swordfish Steak Saute, California Style,
Sliced Cucumbers 65
Chinook Salmon Steak Grilled Mirabeau,
Anchovies Filet 65
Stuffed Half Lobster, Thermidor
Indienne or Americaine 75
Fresh Louisiana Prawns a la Indienne or
Newburg with Rice, Potatoes, Julienne 75

COLD BUFFET SUGGESTIONS
Assorted Hors d'Oeuvres, Paramount Style 85
Stuffed Tomato a la Russ 85
Stuffed Tomato a la Reine 75
Lobster, Crab Meat or Shrimps Louie 75
Breast of Chicken, Isabella 1.00
Chef's Special Half Stuffed Avocado 75
Beef Steak a la Tartar 75

COLD MEATS
Sliced Breast of Turkey 85   Roast Veal 65
Baked Swift's Premium Ham 70
Brisket of Corned Beef 65
Roast Baby Lamb 65   Kosher Pastrami 65
Genuine Virginia Baked Ham 75
Imported Italian Salami 60   Roast Pork 65
Imported Goose Liver Sausage 60
Roast Prime Ribs of Beef 70
Assorted Cold Cut 65
Potato Salad Served with Above Orders

SALADS
1000 Special De Luxe (All Fresh Vegetables,
Choice of Shrimp, Crab Chicken, Avocado or
Lobster) 70
Bartlett Pear and Cottage Cheese 35
Carrots, Apples and Nuts 45   Waldorf 35
California Fruit 60   Combination 50
Pineapple and Cottage Cheese 35
Hearts of Artichoke and Tomato 50
Grapefruit and Avocado 50   Lobster 65
Crabmeat 65   Banana Nut 40   Shrimp 85
Tuna 50   Chicken 60   All White Meat 85
Avocado 40 Melba Peach, Cottage Cheese 35
Grapefruit with Cottage Cheese 35
Special Cottage Cheese Fruit Salad 40
Sliced Tomato 25   Hearts of Lettuce 20
Lettuce and Tomato 35
Sliced Cucumbers 25   Cole Slaw 20
French or Mayonnaise Dressing Served with
All Salads
Sour Cream, Louie or 1000 Island Dressing,
Avocado or Roquefort Cheese Dressing,
10c Extra
Russian Dressing 25c

FROM THE FOUNTAIN
UNTIL 5.30 P. M.

Toasted Deviled Ham Sandwich with
Potato Salad, Coffee 25c

(5c Extra in Dining Room)

Paramount Luncheon
Served from 11:30 A. M. to 2:00 P. M.
40c at Counter   45c in Dining Room
CHOICE OF:
Chicken Gumbo Creole   Chilled Golden Julep
Cook's Salad

Individual Baked Macaroni, Ham au Gratin, Lettuce Salad
Roast Leg of Pork with Dressing, Apple Sauce,
Whipped Potatoes and Carrots Vichy
Scrambled Eggs with Chives on Toast,
French Fried Potatoes and Stewed Tomatoes
Browned Veal Stew with Homemade Noodles and
Baked Squash
Mixed Green Salad with French Dressing
Pineapple Cobbler, Rice Pudding, Jell-O, Pound Cake,
Ice Cream, Stewed Prunes or Sherbet
Tea or Coffee   Hot Rolls   Milk 5c Extra
NO SUBSTITUTES

55c at Counter   60c in Dining Room
Chicken Gumbo Creole   Chilled Golden Julep
Cook's Salad   Seafood Cocktail
Veal Cutlet Holstein with Tomato Sauce, Spaghetti and
New Peas
Steamed Finnan Haddie, New Potatoes in Cream and
Sliced Tomatoes
Roast Tom Turkey with Dressing, Cranberry Sauce,
Candied Yams and String Beans
Tenderloin Steak Saute a la Minute, Sauce Bearnaise,
Baked Potato and Sliced Tomatoes
Assorted Finger Sandwiches with Compote of Stewed Fruit
Pineapple Cobbler, Rice Pudding, Mince Pie, Pumpkin Pie,
Huckleberry Pie, Cocoanut Layer Cake, Ice Cream,
Sherbet, Pound Cake or Jell-O
Tea or Coffee   Hot Rolls   Milk 5c Extra
NO SUBSTITUTES

ENTREES
Entrees marked with Star (*) Ready to Serve

Individual Baked Macaroni, Ham au Gratin,
Lettuce Salad 30
Roast Leg of Pork with Dressing, Apple Sauce,
Whiped Potatoes and Carrots Vichy 40
Scrambled Eggs with Chives on Toast,
French Fried Potatoes and Stewed Tomatoes 35
Browned Veal Stew with Homemade Noodles and
Baked Squash 30
Veal Cutlet Holstein with Tomato Sauce,
Spaghetti and New Peas 50
Steamed Finnan Haddie, New Potatoes in Cream and
Sliced Tomatoes 50
Roast Tom Turkey with Dressing, Cranberry Sauce,
Candied Yams and String Beans 50
Tenderloin Steak Saute a la Minute, Sauce Bearnaise,
Baked Potato and Sliced Tomatoes 50

CHEF'S SPECIAL
Calf's Liver Saute with French Fried Onions, Baked Potato
and String Beans, Hot Rolls, Coffee or Tea 70

SALAD FEATURES
Banana, Pineapple Waldorf Salad with Whipped Cream 30
Romaine, Watercress, Tomatoes and Anchovies with
French Dressing 40
Combination Plate of Chicken Salad, Lobster Salad and
Artichoke Salad 65

SANDWICH FEATURES
Cream Cheese, Date Nut Butter and Raspberry Jam on
Toast, 3-Decker 25
Baked Ham, Jack Cheese, Sliced Tomato, Cole Slaw,
1000 Isle Dressing on Russian Rye Bread 30
Chicken Salad, Avocado, Crisp Bacon, Lettuce on
Toast, 3-Decker 40

Saturday, December 11, 1937

SANDWICHES (Plain or Toasted)
Chicken Salad 25   Chicken 40
Imported Salami 25   Smoked Ox Tongue 25
Baked Ham 20   Minced Ham 15
Roast Beef 20   Nut Relish 20
Peanut Butter and Jelly 25   Tuna Salad 15
Imported Sardine 25   Lettuce, Tomato 20
Avocado 20   Tuna 15   Deviled Egg 15
Pimiento Cheese 15   Club Sandwich 60
American Cheese 15   Domestic Swiss 15
Roast Pork or Veal 20   Ham and Cheese 25
Toasted Cheese 25   Ham and Egg 30
Bacon and Egg 30   Bacon and Tomato 20
Minced Olive 20   Smoked Liver Sausage 20
Philadelphia Cream Cheese 15
Roast Prime Rib 30
Hot Pork, Veal or Beef Sandwich, Pan Gravy,
Mashed Potatoes 30

EGGS AND OMELETS—
MISCELLANEOUS
Boiled Eggs 30   Scrambled Eggs 30
Poached Egg on Toast 35   Plain Omelet 35
Bacon Omelet 50   Tomato Omelet 50
Spanish Omelet 50   Jelly Omelet 50
Chicken Liver Omelet 50   Ham and Egg 50
Bacon and Eggs 45   Sausage and Eggs 50
Fried Egg 30   Scrambled with Tomato 30
Shirred Eggs 35   Ham Omelet 45
Cheese Omelet 50   Poached Eggs, Vienna 60
Poached Eggs, Benedict 65
Welsh Rarebit 60   Golden Buck 65
Yorkshire Buck 75   German Pancake 50
Potatoes, Toast and Jelly Served with
All Egg Orders
(3 Eggs in All Omelets)
All Eggs Scrambled with Pure Cream and
Fried in Butter

POTATOES
French Fried 10   au Gratin 15   Shoestring 10
American Fried 10   Lyonnaise 15
Long Branch 10   Hashed Brown 10
Cottage Fried 15   Baked 15

IMPORTED & DOMESTIC CHEESE
Imported Swiss 25   Roquefort 25
Imported Camembert 25   Domestic Swiss 15
Philadelphia Cream Cheese 25
American Cheese 10   Liederkranz 25
Cottage Cheese with Sour Cream 40

DESSERTS
Huckleberry Pie 10   Pumpkin Pie 10
Mince Pie 10   Rice Pudding 15
Pineapple Cobbler 15   Fruit Cake 15
Cocoanut Layer Cake 15
Strawberry Sundae 15   Pound Cake 15
Ice Cream 10   Compote of Stewed Fruit 30
Fruit Jell-O 10   Cup Cake 05
Cup Custard 20   Doughnut, Each 05
Baked Apple with Cream 20
Compote of Fresh Fruit 40
Chapman's Ice or Ice Cream 10

DRINKS AND BEVERAGES
Tea, Per Pot 10   Cup of Coffee 10
Ice Tea 10   Iced Coffee 10   Buttermilk 10
Cup of Chocolate 10   Postum 10
Certified Guernsey Milk 20
Much to Our Regret, We Cannot be
Responsible for Lost Articles

PARAMOUNT SPECIAL
PLATE

Browned Corned Beef Hash with
Poached Egg, Fresh Spinach,
Hot Rolls, Coffee or Tea 30c

(5c Extra in Dinning Room)

In 1937, diners at the Paramount commissary could choose from tenderloin steak, baked veal, lobster thermidor, Welsh rarebit, and a choice of stewed prunes or sherbet for dessert. Prices peaked at eighty-five cents.

The classic TV series Bonanza *was shot on Paramount's legendary Western Street for most of its long run (1959–1973). The mountain seen here in the back of "Virginia City" was, in reality, a chicken wire and plaster scale miniature, which, unfortunately, birds used to roost on, destroying its illusion of size.*

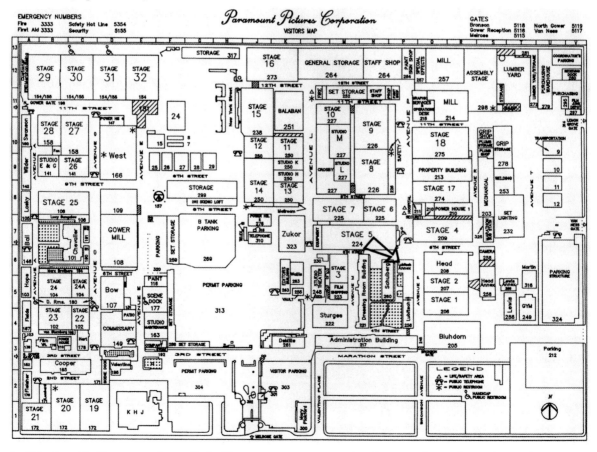

In 1983 a fire robbed Paramount of most of its backlot; temporary structures numbered 24–29 on that year's map show us the approximate location of New York Street, below the still-surviving façades and the location of a temporary rebuild. In 1991 this studio map would be redrawn again with the addition of a permanent New York Street set that survives today (1983 map).

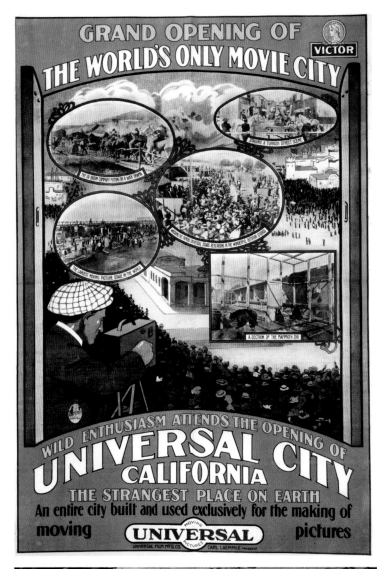

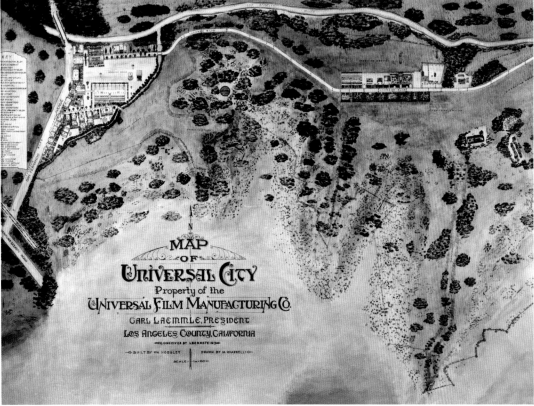

Universal Studios' grand opening on March 15, 1915, was heralded by all the Barnum-style ballyhoo that Hollywood had already seemingly mastered. The actual model map for the operation (below) is somewhat less grandiose than the artist's rendering.

Universal Studios looking north up Lankershim Boulevard into the San Fernando Valley (1916 photo).

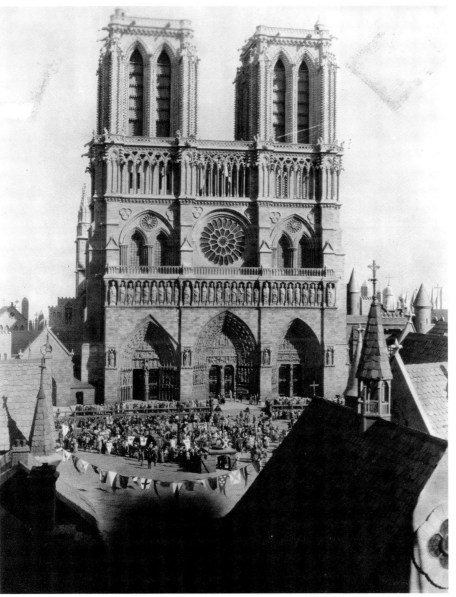

Universal Studios in the 1920s (and for decades after) was primarily known for cheap westerns and comedies. But they did occasionally invest in more lavish "jewel" productions, such as Erich Von Stroheim's Foolish Wives *(1922) and* The Hunchback of Notre Dame *(1923). For the latter, though, most of this Notre Dame cathedral set was a very clever matte painting. Can you spot where the physical set ends?*

Universal's Administration Building (seen here in 1934) once included this Tiffany Glass logo window (2014 insert).

Universal's extensive backlot as it looked in the 1950s.

Fox Films was founded in 1915 by William Fox, who built this studio at 1417 Western Avenue in Hollywood, seen here in 1921 and in this idealized 1929 map.

Fox opened an even larger studio at 10201 West Pico Boulevard in 1928 (1938 photo).

Fox Studio merged with Darryl F. Zanuck's 20th Century Pictures in 1935, which created the familiar logo seen on the roof of the then-property building and at the beginning of thousands of films (1965 photo).

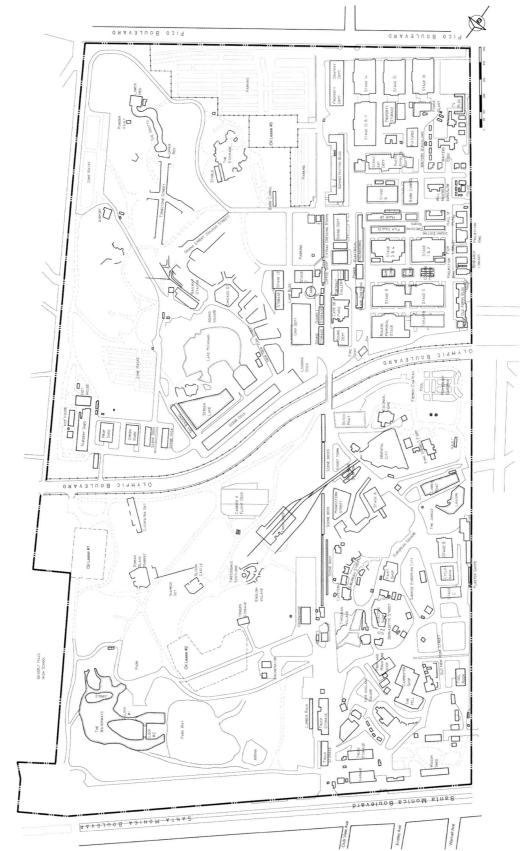

An accurate map of the entire 20th Century Fox studio complex has never been published. This reconstruction was crafted by architect Robert Lane based on several partial or incomplete versions drafted before the studio was fully developed. It represents the entire lot as it looked in the late 1950s — just before almost all of it was sold off.

A young Marilyn Monroe on the "Old New York Harbor Set" on the Fox backlot, shortly after the starlet signed her first, short-lived contract with the studio in 1946.

"The lunatics are running the asylum" was the common quip around town when it was announced that the most powerful and creative people in the industry were starting their own studio in 1919. The result, United Artists, was a powerful new studio that ultimately ended up financing and releasing films that were usually made by others. In 1981 the company would be purchased by MGM. But to the assorted founders, contributors, and hangers-on gathered for a company dinner at the Roosevelt Hotel in 1928, the future must have looked bright indeed.

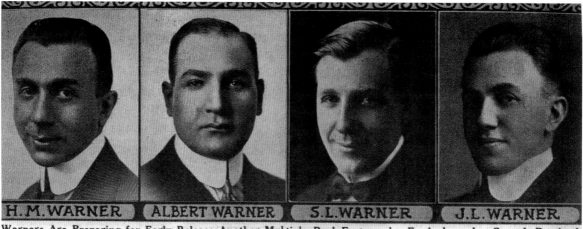

H. M. WARNER **ALBERT WARNER** **S. L. WARNER** **J. L. WARNER**

Warners Are Preparing for Early Release Another Multiple Reel Feature, by Ex-Ambassador Gerard, Destined Become the Logical Successor to "My Four Years In Germany."

All the founding studios were family operations. Disney and Columbia both were founded by brothers, although you wouldn't know it today. Universal had so many family members on the payroll that poet Ogden Nash wryly noted, "Uncle Carl Laemmle has a very large faemmle." But only one company, Warner Bros., brought nepotism into their actual name and logo. Involved in production since the late teens and incorporated in 1923, their success eventually frayed at internal family dynamics, to the extent that all four brothers were seldom pictured together, except in composites such as this one (1919 trade ad).

This ornate colonnade visible from Sunset Boulevard at the original Warner Bros. studio, was like so much else in Hollywood, largely a façade. There were, or are, actual offices behind those doors, but they were shallowly built into the walls of the stage behind, apparently to impress the neighbors (1925 photo).

Much of the original Warner Bros. studio was eventually and indignantly converted into a bowling alley, of all things. Happily, today, movies are again being made on the lot, with Netflix being a key tenant there. Interestingly, the streaming service's recent occupation of the property means that the same stages where talking pictures were innovated is now the home of a company that makes innovative new media for the twenty-first century (1950 advertisement).

In 1928 Warner Bros. acquired a second, much larger studio in nearby Burbank, almost as a byproduct of their purchase of First National Pictures, which had constructed it. The new lot's ample real estate, wide streets, and long, orderly rows of stages made it a perfect location for their expanding empire (August, 1931 photo).

Today Warner Bros. employee identification is accomplished by barcoded photo ID cards, but in past decades numbered buttons like this one were used for admittance by employees, even if they were named Humphrey Bogart or Gig Young (1941 photo).

Warner Bros. Studios in 2020. Perhaps the single-most filmed place on earth.

Walt Disney Studios (incorporated in 1923) operated out of this modest plant in Silver Lake from 1925 until the success of Snow White and the Seven Dwarves *(1937) pushed them into larger quarters (1930 photo).*

Aerial view of the Walt Disney Studios as it looked in the mid-1950s before the construction of the backlot, which a cartoon studio would not have needed. There are, however, already three live-action soundstages visible (bottom right), which perhaps indicate the direction in which the company was already headed.

The eventual Disney backlot included a residential and small-town district, a lake, a "Latin" or "Zorro" Street, and a western town, seen here looking west in this 1967 panoramic reference photo.

The backlot at Disney Studios is long gone, but outdoor sets are still constructed and maintained at the Golden Oak Ranch in Santa Clarita, which the studio has owned since 1959. Here sets for Pirates of the Caribbean: At World's End *are seen under construction (2007 photo).*

Today the Burbank studio includes a "Legends Plaza," where past and current Disney employees are honored. In the background, and with its distinctive Seven Dwarves columns, is the Michael D. Eisner administration building, completed in 1990 (2007 photo).

Columbia Pictures was incorporated under that name in 1924, but founders Harry and Jack Cohn had already been booking and producing films for several years by that point. This 1928 industry ad specifically mentions their new sound recording facilities and "mammoth" stages, which weren't really so mammoth.

The Columbia lot as it looked from Gower Street in 1940 and as it must have looked to the thousands of would-be actors who came in search of fame, most of whom would never see these walls from the other side.

Among the aspiring stars who congregated around Columbia Pictures and its sister studios were many cowboys, actual and would-be, all hoping for a day job as an extra or stunt person on a western that might be shooting inside. Eventually, the intersection of Gower and Sunset, seen here in 1934, acquired the nickname of Gower Gulch due to these buckaroos' sometimes-rowdy presence there. A western-themed strip mall stands on the site today.

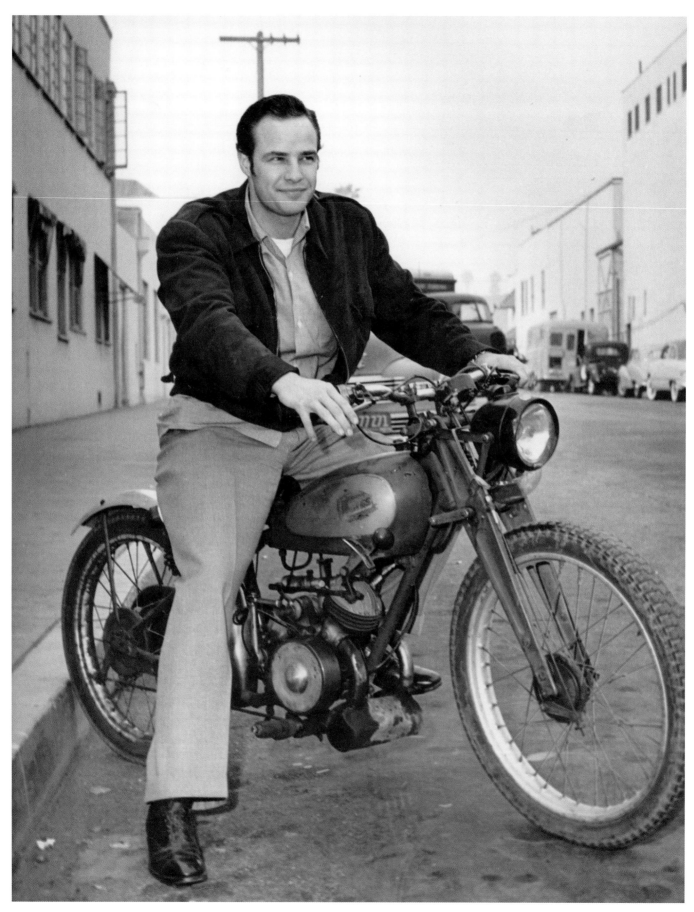

Marlon Brando poses near the Columbia Beachwood Drive gate entrance to Columbia Pictures while shooting, aptly enough, the prototype biker picture The Wild One *in 1953.*

Columbia moved out of its Gower Street lot in 1972 to cohabitate with Warner Bros. in Burbank, and then, in 1990, to MGM's old home in Culver City, seen here in 2010.

Arguably the most famous and legendary of all studios, Metro-Goldwyn-Mayer was founded in 1924 by merging three smaller companies, one of which, Goldwyn Pictures, provided them with this relatively modest but then-modern studio complex in Culver City, seen here looking west in 1925 . . .

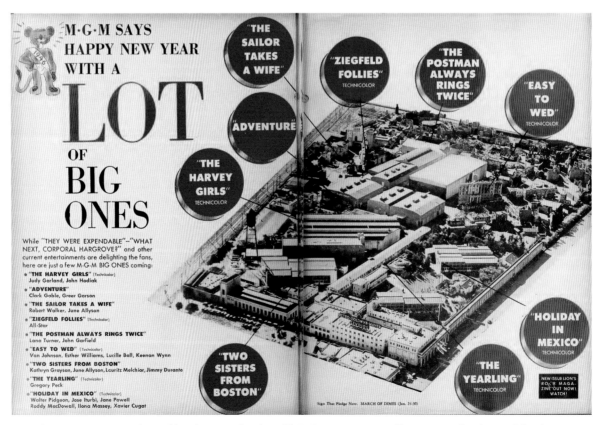

. . . and in 1946, twenty years later, although it seems that the Publicity Department was still using a very dated view of their lot to promote its product, even though the studio then bore very little resemblance to the one in the photo.

Part of the 175-acre MGM in the 1940s, when it had expanded its holdings across Culver City, and across the world.

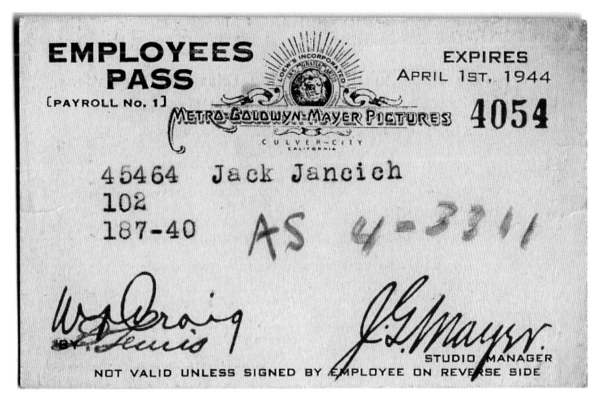

Ticket to a dream factory. Jack Jancich's MGM studio pass. Who was Jack Jancich? (1944 ID card).

Leo the Lion, MGM's legendary mascot/logo appears to have hitched a ride with director Alfred Hitchcock during the production of North by Northwest. *In reality, the director disliked driving a car, and the King of Beasts has been added to create a memorable still photo opportunity (1959 photo).*

Financial concerns pushed MGM out of their longtime Culver City home in 1986. Today the corporation, whose parent company is Amazon, is headquartered in Beverly Hills, a few miles and hundreds of acres away from their romantic past (2018 photo).

Founded in 1929 as a direct result of the sound revolution, RKO (Radio-Keith-Orpheum) Pictures was the last of the major studios of Hollywood's classic era. Their headquarters was at the corner of Melrose Avenue and Gower Street (1949 photo).

The same corner in 1991 after the studio had been absorbed by Paramount.

FORTHCOMING PRODUCTIONS *from* SELZNICK INTERNATIONAL

RONALD COLMAN
in
THE PRISONER OF ZENDA
with

MADELEINE CARROLL

Mary Astor   Raymond Massey
C. Aubrey Smith   David Niven

and

DOUGLAS FAIRBANKS, Jr.

as

Rupert of Hentzau

Direction: John Cromwell

Mark Twain's
THE ADVENTURES OF TOM SAWYER

Direction: H. C. Potter

Rose Franken's
OF GREAT RICHES

Brock Williams'
THE EARL OF CHICAGO

Margaret Mitchell's
GONE WITH THE WIND

Direction: George Cukor

RKO maintained a second studio in Culver City, which they leased to independent producer David O. Selznick, among others (1937 trade ad).

David O. Selznick in his office at "his" studio in 1940. While on the lot, Selznick produced A Star Is Born, Gone With the Wind, *and* Rebecca, *among other legendary films.*

The Selznick-RKO lot in Culver City as seen in 1937. Today Amazon is a primary tenant on the same property.

In addition to David Selznick, other independent producers and companies have maintained their own studios. Seen here in 1987 is the former Samuel Goldwyn lot, although Douglas Fairbanks and Mary Pickford, United Artists, Howard Hughes, Warner Bros., and Oprah Winfrey have also been owners or tenants over the years. Today the plant is generically and aptly known as "The Lot" (1987 photo).

Producer Hal E. Roach proudly shows off his car and his studio in 1921. Roach was responsible for teaming Stan Laurel and Oliver Hardy and discovering or employing dozens of other legendary comedians. The plant would be demolished in 1963, with only a neglected marker in Culver City left today.

Mack Sennett's Keystone Studios, located at 1712 Glendale Boulevard in Edendale, is seen here in 1914. The company ceased to exist in 1935, although some of the buildings pictured here are, rather remarkably, still intact today.

Republic Pictures (seen here in 1962) long operated out of a former, second Mack Sennett property in the aptly named community of Studio City. Most of Republic's output consisted of low-budget westerns and serials, although it must be said that within these genres, they were very good at what they did. Today the studio lot is leased by Viacom/CBS.

st 27

Monogram Pictures was close to the lowest rung on the ladder among film companies that maintained their own roster of stars and technicians and their own studio, specifically this complex in East Hollywood — today a media campus for the Church of Scientology. Inexplicably, French New Wave director Jean-Luc Godard would dedicate his film Breathless (1960) to Monogram Pictures (1941 photo).

Willat Studios of Culver City operated only from 1920 to 1926, but a reminder of its short lifespan is with us today in the form of this unusual fairytale-style house, originally the studio administration building, as seen here (top) in 1921 with studio co-owner Irvin Willat and actress Barbara Bedford. The structure was later moved to Beverly Hills, where it can be gawked at even today (bottom, 2022 photo).

chapter 4

DEPRESSION, WAR, AND POPCORN

HARD TIMES AND BIG AUDIENCES

T he so-called classic studio era, which spanned roughly from 1927 to 1949, is largely when Hollywood defined itself and when the world, in turn, defined Hollywood as a crazy, exotic, crass, and endearing place where pampered stars and put-upon producers worked to make audience dreams come true, if only on the screen.

Off the screen, Hollywood perpetuated and played into these ideas through a perpetual landslide of publicity, fan magazines, posters, and ballyhoo, all designed to sell films, film stars, and the ridiculous industry that had created them. A film's poster represented that movie as its creators wished it to be yet, unfortunately, sometimes isn't, as audiences would find out upon being lured into a theater by its

often-lurid promises. And selling Hollywood was not confined to film posters; publicity stunts, personal appearances by stars, print ads, radio and TV spots, and media junkets all helped to sell the dream—and lots and lots of tickets—to consumers.

It worked beautifully. In the 1930s and '40s, more than 60 million people went to the cinema on an average week. The numbers finally started to drop off after World War II, and since the 1960s have largely flatlined at around ten million (even less, recently). Even so, there is no denying the impact, good or bad, that Hollywood continues to have upon the world, even today.

Even during the "golden era," though, there were fissures that perpetually threatened to erupt and consume the industry and those who depended upon it for employment or entertainment. In Washington, D.C., efforts to break up the monopolistic practices of the big studios always hovered on the horizon, as did a perceived communist threat that would eventually lead to the blacklist. Closer to home, efforts at unionization were long-opposed by studio management. In fact, the Academy of Motion Picture Arts and Sciences, the organization that presents the Academy Awards, was founded in 1927 largely as a way of keeping the industry from unionizing.

It didn't work. In the following decades, contentious and often violent protests, labor efforts, demonstrations, and strikes have brought the studios and the industry to its knees multiple times and exposed a level of corruption, greed, and hubris inherent in Hollywood that usually is ignored by journalists, historians, and fans. World War II and its common and very clear-cut enemy briefly united management and labor, and Hollywood and Washington, in the 1940s. But the truce was, of course, short-lived.

The studios and their stars unreservedly threw themselves behind the war effort by making unabashedly pro-Allied propaganda films for general audiences and producing training films for the troops themselves. Producer Hal Roach, for example, served in the Signal Corps, and his studio lot subsequently became the base of operations for the First Motion Picture Unit—the first Army unit made entirely of filmmakers. Despite the loss of many overseas markets during this era, audiences continued to support movies made for entertainment purposes as well.

As it does today, film poster art in the 1920s and '30s highlighted thrills, action, sex, and stars. Note for example, that Pay Day *(1922) fea-tures Charlie Chaplin exclusively in its advertising; what else was needed? Two aviation epics,* Wings *(1927) and* Hell's Angels *(1930), also highlighted their casts; even though Jean Harlow was not yet a star, the film could be sold on her other attributes. Finally, for* Union Pacific *(1939) the chief selling point was the film's director Cecil B. DeMille, even above that of its well-paid cast.*

*B*IG brute—how they love him! CLARK GABLE took the women of the world by storm because he slapped a girl's face! He is the he-man superb. And there's more to Gable than just that; he is a fine actor and a hard worker. For that reason his hurriedly-won stardom, which might have faded as quickly, will probably last the longer.

M.G.M.

Several examples of the sort of material the studios fed to fan magazines. Mary Pickford christening the "Chinese Dragon" airplane as a publicity stunt at Grauman's Chinese Theatre (1928). Greta Garbo (1928). Clark Gable (1931). And Claudette Colbert sporting her vixen costume as Cleopatra (1934), yet enjoying a wholesome glass of milk.

```
                    Dated:     December 8, 1936

                    Between:   STUDIOS
                                    and
                               PARAMOUNT PICTURES, INC.

                    RKO borrows:  Cary Grant (Actor)

                    Picture:   "THE ROBBER BARONS"

                    Role:      "NICK BOYD"

TERM:   From - NLT Dec. 18, 1936,
        To   - Completion of role, but not less than 8 weeks.

COMPENSATION:  $20,000.00, payable in 8 successive weekly
        installments of $2,500.00 each, commencing 1 week after
        commencement of term.  If after Feb. 6, 1937 actor is
        receiving more than $2,500.00 per week, RKO will also pay
        Universal the sum obtained by multiplying 1/6 of difference
        between $2,500.00 and weekly rate then being paid actor,
        by 4, or such lesser number of days for which RKO may
        require actor after Feb. 6.   RKO will pay for actor's
        services beyond 8-week period at rate of $2,500.00 per week,
        on a pro rata basis, or at such increased rate as actor may
        then be receiving.

CREDIT:  "...agree that the name of the Artist will be co-starred
        or co-featured, as you may elect, with the names of Edward
        Arnold, Frances Farmer and Jack Oakie on the first card of
        the main or credit title of the film and in the cast of
        characters on the screen thereof, and in all advertising
        and paid publicity issued by you or under your control in
        connection with the said photoplay, and that only the name
        of Edward Arnold shall precede, or be displayed in larger
        size of type than that used to display the name of the
        Artist therein, and that the name of the Artist shall be
        displayed in size of type not less than seventy per centum
        (70%) of the size of type used to display the name of
        Edward Arnold therein."

WARDROBE:   RKO to furnish all except modern wardrobe.


                    - - - - -
```

Although for most of his career, Cary Grant was a freelance actor, in 1936 he owed Paramount a picture and therefore was loaned by them to RKO for a film that would later be released as The Toast of New York *(1937). His contract for the assignment specified his character, monetary compensation, wardrobe, and billing.*

Busby Berkeley, the brilliant, innovative choreographer who brought truly cinematic musicals to the screen for the first time, is here watched by chorus girls trying to understand what he is talking about (1933 photo).

Physicist Albert Einstein, on a visit to Hollywood in January 1931, chats with Universal Studios president Carl Laemmle.

Alfred Hitchcock is here at work on his first American movie, Rebecca, *with an intimidated-looking Joan Fontaine. Unlike the director, the writing desk upon which Hitchcock's script sits appears to have already worked on sets all over town (1939 photo).*

Built in 1818, Avila Adobe was the oldest surviving home in Los Angeles, an occasional film location, and a convenient place for Gary Cooper to take a break in the early 1930s.

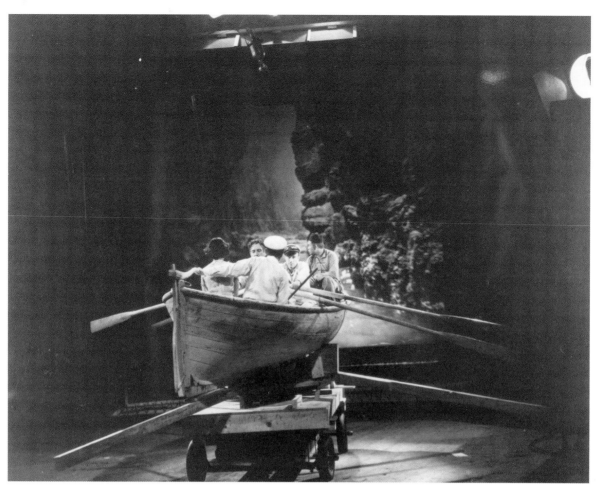

King Kong *(1933) was so successful that a sequel called* Son of Kong *was created and released the very same year. Here Frank Reicher, Helen Mack (with backs to camera), John Marston, Robert Armstrong, and Victor Wong steer a dangerous course in front of a back-projected river on Stage 3 at RKO.*

More trickery. Virginia City *at Warner Bros. (1940 photo).*

More trickery, sort of. Boy Meets Girl *was set in Hollywood, and so staged this shot of James Cagney astride a mechanical horse (1938 photo).*

Gene Autry astride a real horse (Champion) in a real location (Lone Pine, California) for Republic's Comin' Round the Mountain *(1936 photo).*

Henry Fonda uses an electric razor while on location for The Grapes of Wrath *(1940).*

World War II mobilized the country and Hollywood in particular. The Hollywood Canteen, at 1415 Cahuenga Boulevard, offered free entertainment and a chance for servicemen to meet actual stars. Seen above is the venue's opening night, October 3, 1942, and actor Spencer Tracy washing dishes and signing autographs for the troops.

Frank Sinatra entertains servicemen at the Hollywood Canteen (1943 photo).

On the set for "THIRTY SECONDS OVER TOKYO" at M-G-M Studio

A Wac* gets an intimate glimpse of this Metro-Goldwyn-Mayer motion picture production and visits with Van Johnson and
Phyllis Thaxter, who play Capt. and Mrs. Ted W. Lawson, Mervyn LeRoy, the director, and Hal Rosson, the director of photography.

*Women's Army Corps urgently needs you. Join the WAC now!

This ad for MGM's Thirty Seconds Over Tokyo
*(1944) promoted the war effort, and Max Factor's
pancake makeup too.*

PAN-CAKE MAKE-UP originated by MAX FACTOR HOLLYWOOD

Remember, there is only one "Pan-Cake", the original, created by *Max Factor Hollywood* for Technicolor Pictures
and the Hollywood screen stars, and now the make-up fashion with millions of girls and women.

Not all stars were content to serve their country on a soundstage or behind the counter at the Hollywood Canteen. James Stewart and Clark Gable are seen here in their uniforms (1943 photo).

Periodic labor disputes at all the studios were contentious and occasionally violent. Seen here are demonstrations at Paramount (1933), Disney (1941), and Warner Bros. (1946).

Shortly after the war ended, the House Un-American Activities Committee began its investigation into communist activities in Hollywood. Here Eric Johnston, president of the Motion Picture Association of America, and MGM's Louis B. Mayer listen nervously to Jack L. Warner's stammering and ultimately destructive testimony in front of the committee (1947 photo).

Despite Hollywood's obvious moral failings and its ongoing internal strife, its product and its stars remained popular around the world in the postwar era. High Noon (1952), for example, which some saw as an indictment of the blacklist, is here represented by a poster in Israel.

chapter 5

NIGHTCLUBS AND NIGHTLIFE

THE SUNSET STRIP AND HOLLYWOOD'S OTHER DECADENT PLAYGROUNDS

The real estate today known as West Hollywood was originally an unincorporated no-man's-land, a strip of real estate between Hollywood, where many of the stars worked, and Beverly Hills, where many of them lived. Early on, canny entrepreneurs, as well as pimps, bootleggers, con men, and gangsters, realized that money was to be had by starting businesses on and around Sunset Boulevard to lure those commuting celebrities off the straight and narrow. Thus, the legendary Sunset Strip was born. Even today, the Strip is Los Angeles's go-to party zone, as well as a legendary beacon for stars—and for those who try to emulate their lifestyles, if only for a single, expensive, and probably intoxicated evening.

Hollywood's party zone was by no means confined to West Hollywood, but rather included neighborhoods as diverse and far-flung as Malibu, the San Fernando Valley, Beverly Hills, and even downtown Los Angeles. Every luxury hotel, for example, could be expected to offer well-heeled patrons at least one nightclub, lounge, or swimming pool where the good life could be attained and put on display for the rest of the world to admire and/or condemn, sometimes both and at the same time.

It is regrettable indeed, though, that in the twenty-first century, the Strip itself has become the target of developers who are rapidly removing the nightclubs still there and replacing them with million-dollar condominiums and mixed-use high rises, thereby depriving future generations of the vice and sin and intoxicated evenings for which the district is known around the world.

Built in 1903 by H.J. Whitley, the Hollywood Hotel dominated the corner of Hollywood Boulevard and Highland Avenue for decades. Note the Japanese-style house on the hill above the hotel, now the well-known Yamashiro restaurant (1918 photo).

TREASURES FROM THE BISON ARCHIVES

Hotel Hollywood

HOLLYWOOD
LOS ANGELES
CALIFORNIA

AN ALL YEAR ROUND
AMERICAN PLAN HOTEL

*"Not far from where the sea and mountains meet
Where song-birds carol amid fragrant bloom
And breakers dash at our feet."*

AN IDEAL SUMMER AS WELL
AS WINTER RESORT

Wistaria Temple in the Semi-Tropic Garden

It is an interesting sight for the tourist to see the "top"
notchers" of filmland, with sculptors, wielders of the brush,
poets, authors and musicians in little groups here and there
about the spacious lobby and on the tennis court that lies
beside the bowling-green, and partly surrounded by
wistaria and the Cherokee rose that grows in tramp-like
freedom, in the restful atmosphere. There are no trade
winds; but a slight ripple of leaves comes like a lullaby
sound, and blends with the harmony of the Sunday evening concerts.

Hollywood Boulevard Front

Overlooking the Semi-Tropic Garden

Orchid Avenue Corner

There are bridle-paths through the mountains, and can-
yons for the equestrians, and picturesque trails for "hik-
ing." The scenic beauty of the foothills is surpassed by
none in the world and the wonderful boulevards and good
roads leading in every direction make the section a Paradise for motorists and a spot never to be forgotten by
pleasure-seeking travelers.

The picturesque hotel radiates an air of peculiar warmth
and comfort and is apropos of the Golden West.
GEORGE DAVIS, Manager

Main Entrance

The Hotel Hollywood is midway between the center of
Los Angeles and the sea, making it equally convenient to
city and country clubs. It is a fascinating stucco building,
Spanish in architectural beauty, located in a semi-tropic
garden that nestles close to the emerald foothills of Hollywood, the capital of the motion picture world. A beautiful abode for home loving people, tourists, and those of the
different arts. There are sleeping-porches, studio apart-
ments, balconies and wide, shaded piazzas, with cozy
nooks and an attractive sun parlor looking out on a semi-
tropic garden with a riotous bloom of beauty—a charming place for a tête-à-tête when society turns out once a
week for the joys of a dinner dance.

The Palisades at Sunset

Highland Avenue Corner

*The Hollywood Hotel was the first commercial place in Hollywood worthy of a true Hollywood
party. This 1920 brochure highlights the hotel's amenities and ambiance without once mention-
ing the entertainment industry or its members.*

Hollywood Hotel (1944 photo).

Like an aging movie star, the Hollywood Hotel, by the 1950s had become a tired caricature of its former self. This photo was taken in July 1956, just before its pending demolition.

The Hollywood & Highland Center, seen here in 2002 and now known as Ovation Hollywood, stands today on the old Hollywood Hotel site.

Almost across the street from the Hollywood Hotel, and largely financed by movie money, the Hollywood Roosevelt Hotel, seen at the time of its opening in 1929, has never been shy about its industry connections.

The first Academy Award ceremony was held in the Blossom Room at the Hollywood Roosevelt Hotel on May 16, 1929. Although the Academy itself had been created almost two years earlier, no one had thought previously to award prizes to its members.

The famous Tropicana Pool at the Roosevelt has been featured in so many films and television shows that it often seems familiar even to first-time guests (2006 ad).

The Ambassador Hotel, home of the storied Cocoanut Grove nightclub, as it looked in 1926.

With its lush mix of sophistication and exotica, the Ambassador Hotel's Cocoanut Grove nightclub epitomized giddy glamour for generations. Here, in 1929, the formally attired staff seem to welcome us from across the decades. The hotel, the nightclub, and a lot of history would be demolished in 2008.

Having opened in 1912, the Beverly Hills Hotel offered the movie colony stability and old money, neither of which was available in upstart communities like Hollywood (1916 photo).

Basil Rathbone's wife Ouida Bergère arguably threw the most lavish parties in Hollywood during this era, including this masquerade dance at the Beverly Hills Hotel. Bergère is next to her husband, wearing a tiara, near the back and to the left side of the lower level. Violinist Jascha Heifetz, directors King Vidor and Alexander Hall, and actors Adolphe Menjou, Montague Love, and Theda Bara are somewhere in attendance as well, waiting for the next Charleston to start (1929 photo).

The Beverly Hilton Hotel opened in 1955, but it was not until 1961 when it became the home of the Golden Globe Awards that the Hilton was unofficially coronated as a "Hollywood" landmark (1962 photo).

The public never quite seemed to figure it out, but there were several Brown Derby restaurants around Los Angeles and elsewhere. The first, the most famous, and the hat-shaped one on Wilshire Boulevard attracted much of the public's attention, although the one in Hollywood, if less outwardly remarkable, was, perhaps for that reason, more frequented by actual stars and smarmy show business types (top photo 1926, bottom photo 1940).

Hollywood's oldest surviving restaurant, and perhaps the only restaurant on Hollywood Boulevard which still attracts industry attention, the Musso & Frank Grill is known for their legendary martinis. On its centenary in 2019, Musso & Frank became the first restaurant to be given its own star on the Hollywood Walk of Fame (1930 photo).

East of the Sunset Strip, the Earl Carroll Theatre, seen here shortly after its opening in 1938, was famous for its "Reviews" featuring scantily clad showgirls and for a legendary neon sign that bore the memorable phrase "through these portals pass the most beautiful girls in the world" (1938 photo).

An Earl Carroll dinner show "Review" (1940 photo).

In 1968 Earl Carroll's famous neon sign was replaced by the Kaleidoscope logo and "beautiful girls" was slightly modified to read "beautiful people." It was, after all, the 1960s.

Renamed the Aquarius Theatre, Earl Carroll's façade was modified again for the West Coast production of the musical Hair *(1971 photo).*

In 2019 the old Earl Carroll building had its northern wall repainted to match its 1969 look for the film Once Upon a Time in Hollywood *(2023 photo).*

The Sunset Strip looking east into Hollywood proper (1950 photo).

Schwab's Pharmacy, a storied hangout for those waiting to be discovered — and for those in search of those who already had been — could be found across the street (well, almost) from the Chateau Marmont from 1932 to 1983 (1938 photo).

The official gateway into the Sunset Strip is the legendary Chateau Marmont, which has been a haven, a playground, and a hideaway for movie stars and musicians—and for the people interested in partying with them—since 1929 (undated photo).

The girl in the bikini statue seen here (top photo) inexplicably became a beloved local landmark. So much so that in 1961 television producer Jay Ward erected a 14-foot statue of his beloved cartoon character Bullwinkle the Moose across the street and in a similar pose and attire (1956 and 1993 photos).

"When I first drove down the Sunset Strip, I nearly crashed my car gazing at the monolithic ads of various celebrities. They are bigger than King Kong and more frightening," has said actress Rebecca Pidgeon (1997 photo).

Ciro's opened in 1940 and immediately became a go-to spot for celebrities, both on stage and in the audience. Above is a playbill for Mae West's (undoubtedly memorable) 1953 appearance there. Today the building is the home of The Comedy Store (circa 1954 photo).

The western end of the Strip contained smaller, edgier nightclubs, which starting in the 1960s tended to specialize in rock and roll. The most prominent of them was the Whisky a Go Go, seen here as dressed for the 1966 movie The Pad (and How to Use It) *(1966 photo).*

The interior of the Whisky a Go Go is where, supposedly, every rock and roll star since 1964 has performed. Patently untrue, of course. The Beatles, for example, certainly never played there, although all four have as solo artists … so, maybe (1966 photo).

Gazzarri's nightclub was a staple of the LA alternative music scene in the 1960s and '70s. It also featured the popular Miss Gazzarri's Dancers, pictured here, some of whom would achieve a measure of fame on their own (1973 flyer).

The charmingly named Filthy McNasty's Club, like Gazzarri's and the Whisky a Go Go, was a perfect example of the edgier, youth-oriented Sunset Strip of the 1960s. Today the same building, although slated for eminent demolition, is the home of The Viper Room (1969 photo).

In 1966, curfew-related laws on the Sunset Strip designed to keep young people from loitering on the streets after 10 PM eventually led to demonstrations and wide civil unrest which lasted for several months and has since become known as the "hippie riots" (1966 photo essay).

When Tower Records, one of the most influential and important music retailers in the business closed their legendary Sunset Strip store in 2006 it was widely considered to be the end of an era. Pictured here is that store in its glory days and as its fans remember it (1998 photo).

chapter 6

RED CARPETS AND KLEIG LIGHTS

GRAUMAN'S CHINESE THEATRE AND ITS KIN

For roughly the first quarter-century of their existence, most of the major studios owned many of the theaters in which their movies ran. Many of these theaters in Los Angeles and across the country were so elaborate and lavish as to compete with the movies they ran for sheer opulence and spectacle. "I don't sell tickets to movies, I sell tickets to theaters," exhibition magnate Nicholas Loew once remarked.

Hollywood's first premiere was held in 1922 at Sid Grauman's Egyptian Theatre. Since then, velvet ropes, red carpets, shrieking fans, celebrities arriving in limousines, and searchlights scanning the night sky have become almost as synonymous with the entertainment industry as the movies that all the fuss was about. In 1926 Grauman built his iconic Chinese Theatre a few blocks up the road and

the curious tradition of the stars leaving their hand and footprints in wet cement there followed shortly, making the theater both the industry's most desired premiere venue and the most visited movie theater in the world.

Hollywood as illuminated by those familiar Klieg lights in 1965.

Sid Grauman started out in the film exhibition business in San Francisco. After the 1906 earthquake destroyed his theaters there, he salvaged a projector from the ruins, threw up a tent, borrowed some chairs, and the show went on.

By the end of 1917, Sid Grauman had opened a more permanent theater, The Million Dollar, in downtown Los Angeles. The inaugural film to play there, The Silent Man, *would receive a decades-later on-screen shout-out in 1941's* One Foot in Heaven, *in which the earlier film inspires a minister played by Fredric March.*

With an architectural style influenced by the recent discovery of Egyptian King Tutankhamun's tomb, Sid Grauman's Egyptian Theatre became a tourist attraction—and like Grauman himself, was the subject of both postcards and press (circa 1922 postcard).

Grauman was a flamboyantly successful showman who well-realized the value of displaying props from the films that played at his theaters to help bring in the crowds, the largest of which was probably the title character from John Ford's epic western The Iron Horse *(1924 photo).*

Hollywood's most hallowed ritual officially began on April 30, 1927 when Douglas Fairbanks and Mary Pickford (seen here with Sid Grauman) placed their hands and feet in cement inside Grauman's Chinese Theatre's new forecourt. Fairbanks and Pickford have been followed by over three hundred celebrities since then, including eighty-five Academy Award winners, three horses, one lion (Leo), one duck (Donald), two robots (Star Wars), one father and son team-up (Carl and Rob Reiner), and one marionette (Charlie McCarthy).

Grauman's masterpiece and the most famous movie theater in the world is the fabulous Chinese Theatre, here seen being readied for its own premiere in 1927.

On May 18, 1927, Cecil B. DeMille's The King of Kings *became the first film to premiere at the Chinese Theatre. Before the show started, thousands of spectators lined up on Hollywood Boulevard to watch the stars arrive in limousines — a ritual still enacted today.*

More films have premiered at Grauman's Chinese Theatre than in every other theater in the world combined. It has been said, though, that the magnificent, kitschy splendor of the theater's faux-Chinese interiors sometimes has led critics to complain that the best show has not always been to be found up on the screen (1927 photos).

CinemaScope equipment had been installed at the Chinese Theatre in 1953 for the premiere of The Robe *(top photo). In 1956,* The King and I *would follow in the same format (bottom photo).* The King and I *would be reissued in 1961, this time in 70mm — another first for the venue. In 2013 the theater would be adapted to accommodate digital projection and IMAX.*

Warner Bros. Hollywood Boulevard theater opened in 1928 and is allegedly haunted by studio co-founder Sam Warner, who died before it was completed. Today the abandoned, boarded-up theater still stands, with only, perhaps, Warner's ghost, keeping vigil amid its lonely aisles (1928 photos).

The fondly remembered Warner Beverly Hills Theatre is seen here elaborately dressed for the premiere of The Story of Will Rogers *(1952). Insert: A ticket for* A Midsummer Night's Dream *(1935), which also premiered at the theater; note that Max Reinhardt, the film's co-director, is given equal prominence with its "screenwriter" William Shakespeare. The theater would close in 1987.*

Hollywood's Pantages Theatre, seen here both outside (1964) and inside (1953), opened as a movie theater in 1930 and survives today as a live theatrical venue.

The Carthay Circle Theatre, pictured during the 1940 premiere of All This, and Heaven Too, *was one of Los Angeles's most famous theatrical venues due to its unique circular auditorium. The theater would be shuttered in 1969.*

The only concrete geodesic dome in the world, the Cinerama Dome in Hollywood opened on November 7, 1963, for the premiere of It's a Mad, Mad, Mad, Mad World — *the title of which would be tragically borne out two weeks later when President John F. Kennedy was assassinated.*

California's first drive-in theater opened in 1934 at the corner of Pico and Westwood Boulevards. The historic theater would move to a new location in 1944 and remain open until 1973 (1934 photos).

Actress Natalie Wood visits a drive-in and demonstrates how to position a speaker on her car window (1953 photo).

The Victory Drive-In in North Hollywood, which opened in 1949, is seen here in 1968. It would somehow survive until 1977.

chapter 7

TALL WALLS AND TOURISTS

HOLLYWOOD STRUGGLES WITH HOW TO AMUSE ITS ADMIRERS

Travel writers and tourists both have been complaining about Hollywood's rough edges and all-pervasive tackiness for so long that it's hard to feel sorry for anyone who is still surprised by any of it. Visiting modern Hollywood, with its poverty, squalor, and homelessness can undoubtedly be depressing. But if you are of a romantic turn of mind, visiting Hollywood can also be quirky, nostalgic (even if it's your first visit), and emotional. It was producer David O. Selznick who called Hollywood, or maybe it was the idea of Hollywood "the El Dorado of the heart, the soul, and the mind." But let's give it its due as a physical place as well.

Tourism in Hollywood has always depended upon those tourists getting a glimpse of an actual star during their visit. Unfortunately, few stars have ever been willing to spend their days standing on Hollywood Boulevard while smiling and posing for

photos. To make up for this selfish oversight, canny entrepreneurs have designed alternative means for the public to connect with their idols. The most successful of these has been the Walk of Fame, a collection of almost three thousand (and counting) five-pointed stars embedded on the community's sidewalks, each with the name of a star and each available for continuous photo ops to impress the neighbors back home.

Another popular way for star-struck visitors to get close to their heroes is for them to buy a map to, or take a bus tour of, the neighborhoods in which they live. Tourists who do this quickly learn that movie stars, as well as movie producers and movie executives, are able to afford a level of opulence in their personal lives that audiences, especially during the Great Depression, could only dream about. Oddly, the fans who ogle their idols' homes (from a respectable distance, hopefully) or who collect postcards of those homes, rather than resenting their favorites living like gods on Mount Olympus, enjoy living vicariously through those stars . . . which those stars were more than satisfied to do, of course.

Even better, in 1964, Universal Studios decided to throw open its gates and let the public watch those stars on the job. At least that's what they hoped the public would think, although what the studio actually did, brilliantly, was to construct a theme park on their property that was mostly a separate entity from their production facilities. An illusion upon an illusion, that's what Hollywood is all about.

STREET SCENE IN HOLLYWOOD

Thousands buck the line on every call issued for a few movie picture extras. This is a sample of the customary massed assault on the employment bureaus resulting from an ad for a very few men and women to work in an insignificant scene. The wage is meagre for a day or night of hard work.

Don't Try To Break Into The Movies
IN HOLLYWOOD

Until You Have Obtained Full, Frank and Dependable Information

FROM THE

HOLLYWOOD CHAMBER OF COMMERCE
(Hollywood's Great Community Organization)

It May Save Disappointments

Out of 100,000 Persons Who Started at the Bottom of the Screen's Ladder of Fame

ONLY FIVE REACHED THE TOP

An overwhelmed Hollywood Chamber of Commerce was forced to release this handbill in 1931 pleading with would-be stars to not "try to break into the movies in Hollywood." It didn't work.

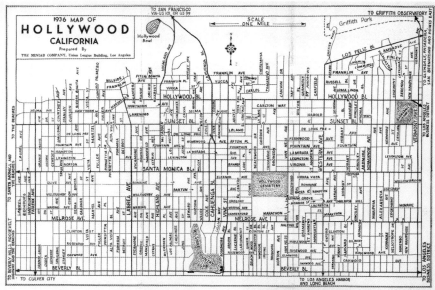

Distances from Hollywood to

NORTH - via U. S. 101		NORTH - via U. S. 101		NORTH - via U. S. 99	
San Francisco	438	Santa Barbara	91	Sacramento	385
Palo Alto	407	Ventura	63	Stockton	337
San Jose	398	Hollywood	0	San Francisco	504
Santa Cruz	376	**SOUTH - via U. S. 101**		Oakland	382
Watsonville	356	Hollywood	0	Manteca	323
Monterey	349	Los Angeles	8	Modesto	348
Carmel	353	Long Beach	31	**Yosemite Park**	
Gilroy	358	Laguna Beach	56	via Merced	354
Salinas	339	Serra (Junction)	68	Merced	276
King City	285	San Clemente	72	Fresno	215
Paso Robles	229	Oceanside	94	Tulare	169
Atascadero	218	Del Mar	112	Bakersfield	106
San Luis Obispo	198	La Jolla	127	Lebec	65
Pismo Beach	185	San Diego	133	Castaic Junction	33
Santa Maria	166	Agua Caliente	153	Hollywood	0
Buellton	135				

HOLLYWOOD BOWL—SEATING OVER 20,000

A tourist's AutoMap of Hollywood. The Las Palmas Hotel, advertised lower left, still exists, and played Julia Roberts's seedy home in the 1990 movie Pretty Woman *(1936 map).*

Tours of stars' neighborhoods have long been a unique only-in-LA industry. Here, an early (1911) tour guide shows some tourists around, and a 1946 starlet offers adventurous motorists maps to their favorite stars' homes.

"Won't the folks back home be jealous!" Hollywood Fantasy Tours offered their guests a city tour from the comfort of a bread-inspired "wonder bus" (1985 photo).

Falcon Lair was the home of screen great Rudolph Valentino. Just across the canyon is where, in 1969, the Charles Manson gang would murder actress Sharon Tate and four others (1925 photo).

Greenacres in Beverly Hills was once the home of silent comic Harold Lloyd (1960s staged photo).

Charlie Chaplin's home on Summit Drive in Beverly Hills (1926 postcard).

Greystone Mansion on Doheny Road in Beverly Hills was built by oil tycoon Edward L. Doheny in 1928. It later became the home of the American Film Institute and was allegedly the inspiration for a location in Raymond Chandler's novel The Big Sleep.

Jack L. Warner's 12,000-square-foot Beverly Hills mansion has since been owned by music executive David Geffen and by Amazon's Jeff Bezos, who paid a record-breaking $165 million for the property in 2020 (1949 photo).

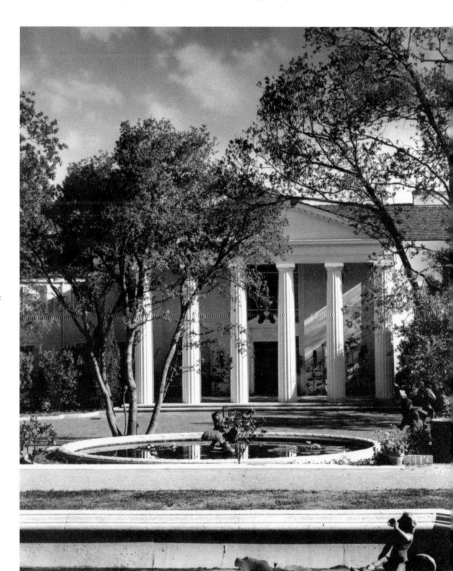

Publisher William Randolph Hearst built this "beach cottage" for his mistress, actress Marion Davies in 1929.

Tom Mix's cowboy chic Beverly Hills estate (1927 photo).

Liberace shows off his piano-shaped swimming pool in Sherman Oaks (1957 photo).

Jack Lemmon barbecues in the back yard of his Hollywood home (1958 photo).

Mae West struts in front of her circular bed inside the Santa Monica estate that she built in 1938.

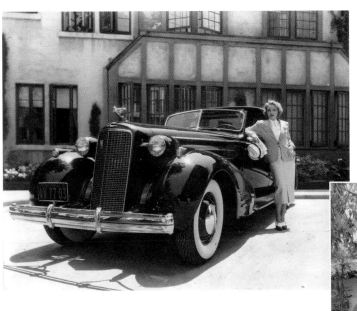

Really lucky fans might get to see their favorite stars in their favorite cars, too. Pictured, Marlene Dietrich with her green Rolls-Royce 1930 Phantom, Clark Gable with his 1936 Duesenberg (a gift from Carole Lombard), Jean Harlow at home with her 1932 Packard Model 903, and Shirley Temple, whose 1935 pedal car may not have been as fast as the others pictured but was surely no less loved.

Tourists who can't be bothered to take a formal tour can always spend a day exploring Hollywood's legendary Walk of Fame, which covers fifteen blocks and includes more than 2,700 stars. Three of those belong to Frank Sinatra, who earned one each for recording, television, and (pictured) movie work (dedicated 1960).

Griffith Observatory (seen here under construction) is almost useless as a portal for viewing the actual stars—the bright lights of Hollywood make that nearly impossible—but popular culture and a different type of stargazing have long compensated for that (1933 photos).

James Dean seen brooding with Griffith Observatory as a potent backdrop in Rebel Without a Cause *(1955), one of dozens of films that have used the observatory as a location.*

Almost since the minute of its opening in 1922, the Hollywood Bowl has been the most famous outdoor amphitheater in the world. Because of its proximity to the entertainment industry (and that industry's vast talent base), it has been estimated that every major celebrity of the twentieth century and beyond has performed on its legendary stage. It might be true, too (1958 photo).

You are cordially invited

to the dedication of

"You Are The Star!"

Mural conceived & painted by

Thomas Suriya

Sponsored by

Playmates of Hollywood

and

City Wide Murals Project

Hollywood Boulevard and Wilcox Avenue

1:00 P.M. - Thursday, September 15, 1983

Music provided by the Hollywood Chorale

Champagne reception immediately

following the dedication

Several murals with Hollywood themes can be found in the district. "You are the star" by artist Thomas Suriya is one of the most interesting in that its perspective is from the point of view of a movie screen, looking into an audience made up entirely of Hollywood legends (1984).

The so-called Hollywood Sign originally read "Hollywoodland," and in 50-foot letters, too, to commemorate the real estate company that constructed it (1923 photo).

By the 1970s the sign, shorn of its last four letters since 1949, was in desperate need of repair…

On November 11, 1978, a rebuilt Hollywood sign was unveiled to great fanfare. Benefactors for the reconstruction included Hugh Hefner, Gene Autry, Alice Cooper, and Andy Williams. Not a single movie studio or television network contributed.

The rarely seen, and not-so-pristine, back side of the Hollywood sign (1993 photo).

Universal was the first studio to offer corporately sanctioned tours of their plant. Here the public watches star Harry Carey and director Fred Kelsey filming Love's Lariat *(1916). The tour would be discontinued with the coming of sound.*

Universal relaunched their tour in 1964, when the public was once again invited through the studio gates to experience firsthand the "entertainment center of the world" (1968 promotion).

Universal's 1967 brochure and a same-era visitors map of their property.

Colorful, fanciful postcards for "Universal City."

Movie magic revealed! A western-themed scenic backing on display for guests (1972 photo).

"Ask for Babs" was an in-joke by director John Landis that involved the fate of a character in his movie National Lampoon's Animal House *(1978).*

AT THE BURBANK STUDIOS — Vip Tour guests experience actual day to day production including shooting on both sound stages, as well as on the many standing outdoor sets. It's a true behind the scenes look into the making of major films and televison programs.

THE BURBANK STUDIOS

4000 Warner Boulevard
Burbank, California 91522

Tours Monday thru Friday
No Children Under 10 Permitted
Blue Room Lunch at extra cost

Reservations Required

CALL (213)

954-1744

Special Rates For Groups

We wish to acknowledge the kind assistance of Warner Bros. Pictures, Warner Bros. Television, Columbia Pictures, Columbia Pictures Television, Orion Pictures Company, The Ladd Company and Lorimar Productions in producing this brochure and, too, for helping to make TBS Tours possible.

Design by Atkin & Co.

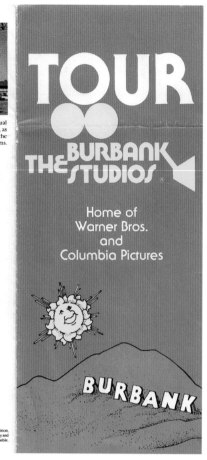

TOUR

THE BURBANK STUDIOS

Home of
Warner Bros.
and
Columbia Pictures

BURBANK

Universal's amusement park has always been the most ambitious "studio tour," but other film companies have opened their gates to guests at various times as well. Above is promotional literature for The Burbank Studios (Warner Bros.) (1980), Paramount (1990), and Warner Bros. again (1992).

Time Frame
A STUDIO TOUR

WARNER BROS. STUDIOS

VIP TOUR

VIP STUDIO TOUR

In a town known the world over for excitement and glamour, a town where celebrities can be seen almost everywhere you go, Warner Bros. Studios is more than ever a special place where movie magic is an everyday occurrence. Recently rededicated as the home of Warner Bros. Pictures, Warner Bros. Television, and Lorimar Television, Warner Bros. Studios is bustling with movie and television production. The star system has waned, but the Warner Bros. galaxy of stars continues to shine: Chevy Chase, Clint Eastwood, Morgan Freeman, Mel Gibson, Danny Glover, Michael Keaton, Danny DeVito, Michelle Pfeiffer, Jack Nicholson, and Jessica Tandy have lent their talents to such memorable films as the *Batman* films, *Dirty Harry* series, the *Lethal Weapon* thrillers, the *Vacation* movies, and *Driving Miss Daisy.*

Reservations are required,
but last minute plans
can often be accommodated.
Visa and Mastercard accepted.
For Tour availability and details
please call **(818) 954-1744.**

Because our Tour visits working areas, children under ten years of age are not allowed.

Warner Bros. Studios Tour
*4000 Warner Boulevard
Burbank, California 91522*

chapter 8

AROUND TOWN AND DOWNTOWN

OTHER LOS ANGELES LANDMARKS: FREEWAYS, WHIMSY, AND KITSCH

Lionos Angeles isn't just about Hollywood. Although it may seem like it to those who have never been there. Or to those who have only been there once. The truth is, Los Angeles is Hollywood, and Hollywood is Los Angeles. Director John Ford once admitted that "Hollywood is a place you can't geographically define. We don't really know where it is." And John Ford was right. Because even Los Angeles's non-cinematic attractions usually turn out to have been used as locations or inspirations for film, TV, or music endeavors. The city's seemingly unrelated industries, like aviation, technology, and real estate often somehow seem to dovetail back into Hollywood as well.

That said, Los Angeles County sprawls over an almost unimaginable 4,751 square miles (by contrast, New York City in its entirety is only 300 square miles). And Los Angeles County boasts a population of almost ten million people, much greater than that of most entire American states. So, there is a lot of man-made real estate there to explore even without Hollywood.

And it's almost all within the Thirty-Mile Zone, too.

From 1901 to 1961 Los Angeles, nearly in its entirety, could be traversed on the Pacific Electric Railway company's "Red Cars" (1947 and 1952 photos).

In 1988 the well-remembered Red Cars were nostalgically recreated for the film Who Framed Roger Rabbit, *which satirized the construction of the city's freeway system, which would be instrumental in the eventual fate of the Red Cars.*

Dozens of Red Cars stacked and awaiting imminent destruction (1954 photo).

Los Angeles City Hall, seen here under construction in 1927, was the tallest building in the city for many years due to height restrictions imposed upon other builders by City Hall.

City Hall has always been a magnet for film productions. One of its earliest appearances was in While the City Sleeps, *where it attempted to upstage (unsuccessfully) star Lon Chaney (1928 photo).*

"Between the city and the sea." In October 1906 an organization known as the Rodeo Land and Water Company started subdividing and selling parcels of land in a district that they named after Beverly Farms, Massachusetts. Although a success, Beverly Hills would not be incorporated until 1914. Prices for lots in the city have gone up since then, too.

Neither as large nor as famous as the nearby Hollywood sign, its modest cousin in Beverly Hills also predates it, having been built in 1907. The version that tourists photograph today is actually a decades-after-the-fact copy of the original, photographed here in 1915.

Another early version of another famous Beverly Hills sign greets visitors entering the expensive community from the east in 1939.

THE PALMS OF BEVERLY DRIVE

The so-called "palms of Beverly Drive" were already attracting attention when this ad was published in 1920. By the time the street became a location for the popular 1960s TV series The Beverly Hillbillies, *however, those palms had grown considerably taller.*

BEVERLY HILLS

A Masterpiece of City Planning

THE miraculous growth of Beverly Hills is following closely a wise plan devised before the city itself was founded. This controlled development of the entire city insures forever the finest type of home surroundings for your family and promises a steady increase in the value of your investment here.

Every street in Beverly Hills is a veritable colonnade of beautifully designed homes with wide parkways and a consistent planting scheme that lends distinctive charm to each well shaded avenue. The palms of Beverly Hills are world famous and the curving boulevards produce vistas of beauty that can never be achieved in less skillfully planned communities.

Consistent adherence to the splendid city plan of Beverly Hills is a fixed policy of the city government under a board of leading citizens who gladly serve their city without pay. The future of this city is safe in their hands. Your home deserves the kind of protection it will always receive in Beverly Hills.

Los Angeles has always been a haven for whimsical, eccentric people—and whimsical, eccentric novelty architecture. From top, a chili stand in Hollywood (1934), an ice cream shop on Beverly Boulevard (1932), a sphinx-shaped real estate office in West Hollywood (1929), and a hot dog stand on the corner of La Cienega and Beverly Boulevard (1953). Only the last, the Tail O' the Pup, still exists today, albeit in a different location.

Westwood Village, on the edge of the University of California Los Angeles (UCLA) campus, was and is a popular shopping destination (1940 guidebook).

Venice, California—modeled, rather obviously, after Venice, Italy—as it looked in 1907.

Completed in 1939, the Streamline Moderne May Company Building on Los Angeles's "Miracle Mile" district is now the home of the Academy of Motion Pictures Museum (photo circa 1950s).

Santa Monica Boulevard in West Hollywood looking north up Doheny Drive. On the far right is the famous Troubadour nightclub where many famous bands have been discovered (1962 photo).

The Los Angeles Farmers Market opened in 1934 and continues to be a popular destination today for both tourists and locals (1958 photo).

Gilmore Field, which stood next to the Farmers Market (and where CBS TV Center is today) was the home of the Hollywood Stars minor league baseball team. The stadium would be demolished in 1958.

Dodger Stadium during its construction in 1959… and in 2002.

The Los Angeles Memorial Coliseum has hosted the Summer Olympics twice and has been featured in films starring Buster Keaton, Charlton Heston, Warren Beatty, Kurt Russell, and Charlie Sheen, among others (1960 photo).

Los Angeles International Airport was originally called Mines Field (after real estate agent William W. Mines). Its iconic Theme Building is a landmark of Googie, or futuristic, architecture (1923 exposition ad and 1963 photo)

Malibu Pier in 1940 and Santa Monica Pier in 1986.

Pacific Ocean Park was a Santa Monica amusement park built south of the current Santa Monica Pier in 1958 to potentially compete with Disneyland. The park would close in 1967 (1961 photo and 1963 admission ticket).

Disneyland's Sleeping Beauty Castle as it looked the year after the park's opening. Ironically, Disneyland's design and aesthetic were heavily influenced by Hollywood set construction techniques (1956 photo by William Wanamaker).

Several major studios are located near cemeteries. Both Warner Bros. and Disney sit behind Forest Lawn, and what would become Paramount, pictured here, was initially carved out of the southern end of Hollywood Cemetery (circa 1926 photo).

Grief-stricken fans and members of the press gather at Westwood Memorial Cemetery for the funeral of Marilyn Monroe on August 8, 1962.

chapter 9

RADIO, MUSIC, AND TELEVISION DAYS

HOLLYWOOD GETS INTO THE MUSIC BUSINESS AND TV RIDES TO ITS RESCUE, AT A PRICE

Radio was considered a frightening and potentially dangerous business to Hollywood in its early days. Eventually, however, most of the studios, especially Warner Bros., embraced the new technology and many of the most iconic song recordings in history would ultimately be created in Hollywood. Some of these songs or orchestral pieces were associated with movies or with labels owned by movie studios. Others came—and come—from powerful independent labels like Capitol, Virgin, and Interscope, all of which are based in Los Angeles.

The transition into television production was more contentious. Television had been predicted as far back as the 1920s but it wasn't until after World War II that the "one-eyed monster" started widely appearing in American homes and keeping American homeowners away from American theaters. The studios, imagining television as an enemy that would destroy their business model, came up with assorted, colorfully named gimmicks (3-D, CinemaScope, Todd-AO, Cinerama) to lure their former patrons back.

As it turned out, television would not be the destroyer but rather the savior of Hollywood. Today the vast majority of Los Angeles's more than four hundred soundstages are now used to produce television or streaming programming, providing employment for thousands of above and below-the-line workers.

Movie goddess Gloria Swanson rather tentatively faces the microphone for a 1927 radio appearance.

Warner Bros. radio station KFWB originally broadcast from their studio on Sunset Boulevard, which reportedly interfered with the recording of sound movies there. Consequently, the transmittal towers would be relocated atop the Warner Hollywood Theatre on Hollywood Boulevard (hand-tinted 1949 photo).

COLUMBIA   BROADCASTING   SYSTEM
LUX RADIO THEATRE
1615 NORTH VINE—HOLLYWOOD

No. 399

FEBRUARY

13

1950

PHOTOPLAY MAGAZINE
1949 GOLD MEDAL AWARD WINNER

James Stewart   June Allyson
in
"THE STRATTON STORY"

WILLIAM KEIGHLEY

CHILDREN UNDER TWELVE WILL NOT BE ADMITTED

CBS

MONDAY
6-7 p.m.
Doors Close
at 5:50 p.m.

In the 1940s and '50s it was common for movie stars to perform in radio adaptations of their recent films. So, in 1950 the holder of this ticket could have seen, and heard, James Stewart and June Allyson recreate their Stratton Story *roles live for the microphone.*

Completed in 1956, the Capitol Records Tower, adjacent to the famous corner of Hollywood and Vine, was the first circular office building in the world and well-symbolized the relationship between the recording and film industries. On the roof, a spire blinks out the word "Hollywood" in Morse code. Inside, many of the legendary songs of the twentieth century and beyond have been crafted and recorded (1957 photo and album cover).

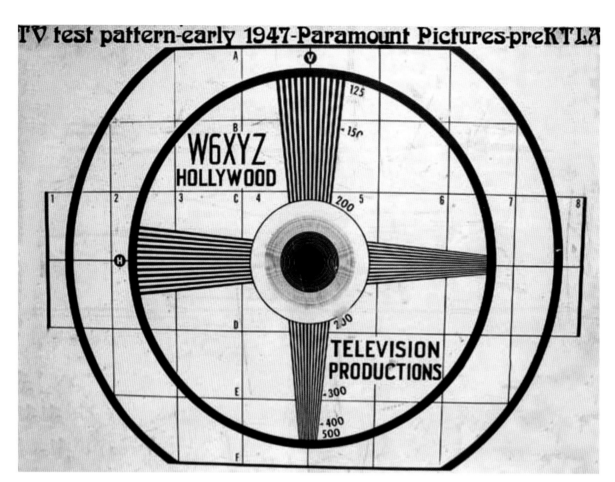

KTLA (W6XYZ), which was once based on the Paramount lot, was the first commercial television station on the West Coast when it began broadcasting in 1942. This is their actual 1947 test pattern.

For anyone who wanted to purchase a television in the 1940s, their options were as limited as the programming was. Customers in the Dick Baird appliance store at 5974 West Pico Boulevard could have seen these models there in 1949, however.

KTLA was originally affiliated with the fledgling DuMont Network, which produced this striking neon sign, circa 1950.

Behind the scenes at a DuMont Network vaudeville review program. Note the female technicians in 1946!

William "Hopalong Cassidy" Boyd was a washed-up former cowboy star when he got the idea of licensing his old movies for television. The stunt paid off to the extent that he began producing new episodes for the fledgling NBC network and in 1950 made the cover of both Time and Life magazines.

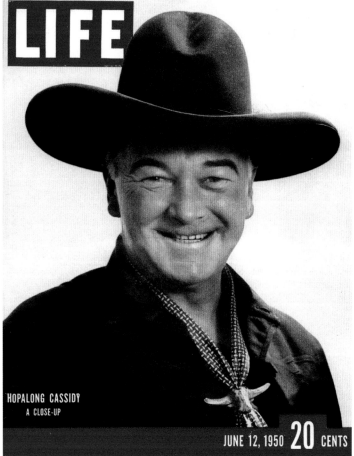

Hollywood on Television *(1949–1952), which aired on KLAC TV, starred a young Betty White.*

CBS Columbia Square opened in Hollywood in 1939 as a radio studio. The network continued to operate out of the facility until they moved to larger quarters in Studio City and in West Hollywood (1939 photo).

Elvis Presley in the parking lot of the CBS Television City complex (circa 1958).

Carol Burnett behind the scenes on her long-running (1967–1978) variety show which shot at CBS's Television City.

ABC was long based out of the old Vitagraph Studios lot in East Hollywood. Today the plant is owned by ABC's parent company, Disney.

Walt Disney (seen here with dolls representing Mickey Mouse, Goofy, and Peter Pan) was the first movie studio boss to align himself with television, specifically with ABC, which he produced content for, and which in turn helped him to finance the construction of Disneyland in 1954.

NBC's original Los Angeles studio, their "West Coast Radio City" was located at Sunset Boulevard and Vine Street (1949 photo).

NBC completed their move to a newer, larger studio in Burbank, their "Color City Studios," in 1952. Today NBC is based on the Universal lot, and this studio is owned by Warner Bros. (1952 photo).

NATIONAL BROADCASTING COMPANY, INC.

COLOR CITY

3200 OLIVE AVENUE, BURBANK

(See Map on Reverse Side)

STUDIO

4

● SUNDAY

● DEC. 1, 1957

● 6:00 to 7:00 PM

Doors Close at 5:40

The Dinah Shore Chevy Show

WITH DINAH'S GUESTS

Rossano Brazzi

Ted Reid   *Pat Suzuki*

AND SPECIAL GUEST

Jimmy Durante

● In Living Color   Children Under 12 Not Admitted

Ticket to watch the taping of a 1957 episode of The Dinah Shore Show *(1951–1957) at "Color City."*

All the movie studios eventually and profitably made their facilities available to produce television. Here the television series Batman *(1966–1968) uses the Culver Studios lot and* That Girl *(1966–1971) shoots at Paramount.*

chapter 10

AUCTIONS, PIXELS, AND PERCENTAGES

HOLLYWOOD GOES CORPORATE AND A NEW GENERATION OF FILMMAKERS CALLS THE SHOTS

As ticket sales and profits continued to shrink, both David O. Selznick and 20th Century Fox started selling off their physical assets and real estate in the 1950s and '60s. The most telling symbol that an era had truly ended was in 1970 when MGM—long acknowledged as the most prestigious movie studio in the world—opened its gates to the public and sold everything from *The Wizard of Oz's* ruby slippers to a full-size Mississippi paddle wheeler to the highest bidder. This eventually led to the fabulous sums now commanded at auction for movie/TV-related props, costumes, and ephemera.

Meanwhile, a newer, younger generation of moguls and movie stars arrived to supplement and eventually replace those who had come before. In the 1970s when films like *The Godfather* (1972) and *Jaws* (1975) proved that single movies could gross hundreds of millions of dollars at the box office, conglomerates like Gulf+Western, which had bought Paramount Pictures in 1966, realized that a studio could be profitably and corporately run as a big business enterprise.

The studios and the star system, and the stars themselves—at least a few of them—still survive today. But in the twenty-first century, sequels, tentpole franchises, and cinematic universes are more attractive to audiences and studio accountants than any single film or actor. Even so, the mystique of the movies, of the movie star, and of Hollywood itself survives.

Considered to be the first of the "new stars," although he has now been dead for more than sixty years, was James Dean, seen here with costar Natalie Wood on the set of Rebel Without a Cause. *Dean's star blazed like a fiery comet ever so briefly before his death in 1955 left a generation feeling alienated and betrayed (1955 photo).*

Even as much of Hollywood's product appeared increasingly outdated and quaint to youthful audiences, occasionally studio films managed to subvert the system even while working within it. Orson Welles' Touch of Evil (1958, seen shooting on location on Windward Avenue in Venice, CA), and Alfred Hitchcock's Psycho (1960), for example, were both artistic and scary.

Sammy Davis Jr., who lost one of his eyes in 1954, here picks out a glass replacement for his role in Johnny Cool *(1963 photo).*

Steve McQueen, one of a new breed of antihero superstars as seen in one of his biggest hits Bullitt *(1968 photo).*

The legendary MGM auctions, held in April and May of 1970 proved to be both a symbolic and a literal end of an era for Hollywood. Actress Debbie Reynolds reportedly spent $180,000 buying everything she could snatch up. But most of the costumes, for example, were ultimately sold in rummage bins for a dollar an item. Many of these same pieces have sold at subsequent auctions for hundreds of thousands of dollars each.

Alex in Wonderland *(1970) featured a movie-within-a-movie scene that MGM expensively staged on Hollywood Boulevard in front of larger crowds than would later attend the movie. Larry Edmunds Bookshop can be seen on the right amid the controlled chaos.*

James Caan, Marlon Brando, director Francis Ford Coppola, and Al Pacino on the set of The Godfather *(1972), which proved that Hollywood's new handlers could produce and market successful, creative films for a new era.*

Mel Brooks, playing an Indian(!), has his warpaint touched up for Blazing Saddles *(1974 photo).*

The last tycoon. One of Paramount's founders, Adolph Zukor, still on the lot at the age of one hundred, aided by Fritz Hawkes, his favorite security guard (1974 photo).

Jaws (1975) was the first true summer blockbuster. Here director Steven Spielberg clowns uneasily with his star on location.

The title role in The White Buffalo *(1977) was played by a bovine-shaped robot that moved on a concealed track and upstaged costar Charles Bronson.*

Margot Kidder and Christopher Reeve flying high on the set of Superman *(1978 photo).*

JULIE ANDREWS STAGE 2

Julie Andrews

Mary Poppins
filmed here
June – September 1963

The Princess Diaries
filmed here
October – December 2000

In recent years the major studios have become more aware of their star-studded histories, as reflected by these plaques which have, most belatedly, been installed on their sound-stage's walls. Warner Bros. and Paramount have left spaces to (hopefully) honor any future masterpieces filmed inside, but Fox is apparently less optimistic, and Disney has chosen to recognize only one of their favorite stars by naming the entire stage after her.

Paramount STAGE 16
Constructed 1941

Features

YOU'RE NEVER TOO YOUNG	1955	LOOKING FOR MR. GOODBAR	1977		
THAT CERTAIN FEELING	1956	FOUL PLAY	1978		
DESIRE UNDER THE ELMS	1957	PRETTY IN PINK	1986		
ROCK A BYE BABY	1957	SHE'S HAVING A BABY	1988		
THE JOKER IS WILD	1957	STAR TREK VI: THE UNDISCOVERED COUNTRY	1991		
HOUSEBOAT	1958	STAR TREK: INSURRECTION	1998		
VERTIGO	1958	ELIZABETHTOWN	2005		
FIVE PENNIES	1959	MISSION: IMPOSSIBLE 3	2006		
THE ERRAND BOY	1961	LARRY CROWNE	2010		
HATARI	1962	DINNER FOR SCHMUCKS	2010		

Television

STAR TREK VOYAGER	1995-2001				
MTV VIDEO AWARDS	2008				
GLEE	2010-				

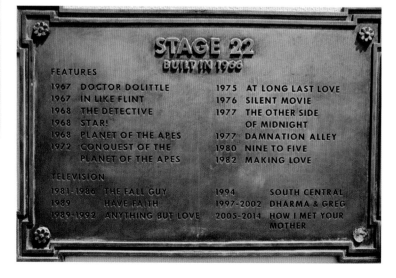

STAGE 22
BUILT IN 1966

FEATURES

1967	DOCTOR DOLITTLE	1975	AT LONG LAST LOVE
1967	IN LIKE FLINT	1976	SILENT MOVIE
1968	THE DETECTIVE	1977	THE OTHER SIDE OF MIDNIGHT
1968	STAR!		
1968	PLANET OF THE APES	1977	DAMNATION ALLEY
1972	CONQUEST OF THE PLANET OF THE APES	1980	NINE TO FIVE
		1982	MAKING LOVE

TELEVISION

1981-1986	THE FALL GUY	1994	SOUTH CENTRAL
1989	HAVE FAITH	1997-2002	DHARMA & GREG
1989-1992	ANYTHING BUT LOVE	2005-2014	HOW I MET YOUR MOTHER

The long-gestating Academy Museum of Motion Pictures finally opened in 2021. Seen here is its eye-catching David Geffen Theatre, which was built into the back of the historic May Company Building, which is pictured in its previous incarnation on page 182 (2024 photo).

On display at the Academy Museum: Bruce the shark, from Jaws (1975), and Rosebud the sled, from Citizen Kane (1941).

The most hallowed totems of old Hollywood, however, surely remain the ruby slippers from The Wizard of Oz *(1939). This screen-used pair was sold at the MGM auctions in 1970 and has been on display at the Smithsonian Institution since 1979.*

A second pair of ruby slippers, also screen-used, was donated to the Academy Museum by a consortium of benefactors, including Leonardo DiCaprio and Steven Spielberg, for the museum's 2021 opening.

Notable survivors of an earlier era include Sid Grauman's Chinese and Egyptian theaters. The Chinese is now owned by TCL Technology, a Chinese-based electronics company. With equal irony, the Egyptian now belongs to Netflix, which boasts of a business strategy intended to bypass theatrical exhibition entirely (2023 photos).

The two-thousand-seat Orpheum Theatre in downtown Los Angeles, now restored, is another very lucky reminder of a more romantic era (1931 and 1989 photos).

Hollywood itself, looking north up Vine Street (1976 photo).

The rituals continue. Pictured is the 2016 Academy Awards, presented at the Dolby Theatre, a few yards and eighty-seven years away from where the same ceremony was first held in 1929.